a good day to die

Inside a Suicidal Mind

by

Mahita Vas

Marshall Cavendish
Editions

Published in 2021 by Marshall Cavendish Editions
An imprint of Marshall Cavendish International

A member of the
Times Publishing Group

Other Marshall Cavendish Offices:
Marshall Cavendish Corporation, 800 Westchester Ave, Suite N-641, Rye Brook, NY 10573, USA • Marshall Cavendish International (Thailand) Co Ltd, 253 Asoke, 16th Floor, Sukhumvit 21 Road, Klongtoey Nua, Wattana, Bangkok 10110, Thailand • Marshall Cavendish (Malaysia) Sdn Bhd, Times Subang, Lot 46, Subang Hi-Tech Industrial Park, Batu Tiga, 40000 Shah Alam, Selangor Darul Ehsan, Malaysia

Marshall Cavendish is a registered trademark of Times Publishing Limited

National Library Board, Singapore Cataloguing-in-Publication Data

Names: Vas, Mahita.
Title: A good day to die : inside a suicidal mind / by Mahita Vas.
Description: Singapore : Marshall Cavendish Editions, 2021. | Includes bibliographic references.
Identifiers: OCN 1244800111 | ISBN 978-981-4974-26-4
Subjects: LCSH: Vas, Mahita—Mental health. | Suicidal behavior—Singapore—Psychological aspects. | Manic-depressive persons—Singapore.
Classification: DDC 616.858445—dc23

Printed in Singapore

For Debbie Fordyce & Ylita Garland

Foreword

A number of similar posts appeared on my news feed one morning in August 2020. The first line read, "There were a total of 400 reported suicides in Singapore in 2019 ...", followed by another, "Youth suicides still a concern, with 94 cases last year ...", and I finally stopped scrolling when this headline hit me, "Suicide remains leading cause of death for those aged 10 to 29 in Singapore ..." Horrified, I clicked to read the report.[1] The figures were released as part of a highly publicised campaign by Samaritans of Singapore to introduce a text-based service for anyone in distress and contemplating suicide. The report, presented as a fact sheet and devoid of emotion, provided a clearer picture of the numbers: a total of 400 suicides, of which 94 were youths, which included 71 who were between the ages of 20 and 29. Noticeably, the report omitted the actual figures for the suicides of the younger group, but a quick calculation showed that, of the 94 youths who killed themselves, 23 were between the ages of 10 and 19. I froze, staring at the numbers, feeling numb.

---

1   Samaritans of Singapore (SOS) Media Release, August 2020

The sobering effect of the report piqued my curiosity and I was keen to learn how Singapore compared with the rest of the world. According to the World Health Organisation,[2] globally, nearly 800,000 people kill themselves every year – one person every 40 seconds. Suicide is the leading cause of death in young people between the ages of 15 and 19. For every suicide there are many more people who attempt suicide every year. A prior suicide attempt is the single most important risk factor for suicide in the general population.

I had never bothered with suicide statistics, but reading of a ten-year-old's suicide in Singapore troubled me deeply. I searched for information – his background, his circumstances – but could not find any. In the process of looking, I learnt about another young boy who had committed suicide by jumping off the 16th floor of a building. He was only 11 years old and had been battling clinical depression. I read about how his mother coped with his sudden and unexpected death, and was in awe of a woman who, battling depression herself, had recognised the signs and sought help for her son years earlier.

I thought about the pain and anguish my late mother would have had to deal with had I been successful with my attempt 15 years ago. I thought about my husband and children, who might still be carrying the scars. I do not think anyone ever really comes to terms with a loved one wanting to, and choosing to, die.

For most people, certainly everyone I know, being alive is something they either take for granted, or treasure as a precious gift. For the faithful, it is a bountiful blessing. Being alive means soaking up experiences on any day. Like basking in the warmth

2   World Health Organisation Fact Sheet / Detail / Suicide September 2019

of a sunny day after days of torrential rain, or admiring the varied hues and shapes of vegetables at the market, or savouring every mouthful of a meal, whether at a hawker centre, at home or in a restaurant, or hugging someone... the little things that remind us all that life is precious, and something to value. Death is something to stave off, perhaps even to fear.

For me, being alive often feels the same as it does for most people. But, sometimes, I contemplate death not only as an option, but as salvation. Having survived a prior suicide attempt, I am considered a risk factor for suicide in the general population.

In Singapore, if you or someone you know is suicidal, please call 1800 221 4444 for help. If someone is in immediate danger, please call 999.

In other countries, please call your local emergency number.

Chapter 1

I have had a morbid fascination with death since I was in my teens. Specifically, suicide. It was not as if I needed to run away from hardship. My mind simply gravitated towards stories about death; murder and suicide were topics of great interest to my young mind. It seemed natural to me, and I never thought to question my preference. It helped that there were always enough such stories in the newspapers to keep me entertained. With every suicide report I read, I wondered what it would feel like, standing at the top of a block of flats, and jumping to my death. It did not horrify me to think of such a violent death. The local broadsheet was particularly good for international news which was not limited to politics, and sometimes reported on gruesome murders in a village in some distant land. Captivating as some of the stories were, I would feel angry if the killers were not caught, and equally happy if they were, especially if they were killed.

By the time I was in my early twenties, I had become aware of my suicidal thoughts and was increasingly keen on suicide as a subject. My job as a stewardess took me to cities which were often shut on weekends, leaving little to do except to read, watch movies in the hotel or at the cinema. Between the books and newspapers I had read, and the movies I had watched in the eighties, there were countless instances of suicide. The reasons varied and included heartbreak, mainly women, but men too; threats from loan sharks; bullying, mostly in Japan back then; and in very few instances, despair so profound that the character needed medical intervention. All the reasons for suicide seemed normal to me. It also seemed normal when no reasons were offered for a particular suicide.

For decades, I had resisted many lifestyle choices, including exercising and managing my high-carbohydrate diet. It seemed pointless to make an effort when I could not see myself living long enough to reap the benefits. Long before I had written my first book, I had thought about writing a novel, but did not go any further than thinking up a plot. It did not make sense to me, starting on something when I was probably going to kill myself before the book was finished.

It was around that time when I started to think about choosing to die my way, and at a time I chose, as being normal. I never discussed it with anyone because people always seemed to discuss suicide like it was a terrible thing. The general belief was that suicide was a great sin and a despicable act by a selfish and thoughtless person. Such souls would surely rot in hell, they would say. Yet, all I could see was an appealing exit if and when I needed one. What I could not see, and did not even consider, was why I would even need to plan my exit. Yes, it was attractive to be able to kill myself when I wanted to, but why on earth would I even want to? I did not think to ask myself this question until much later, after I was diagnosed with bipolar disorder.

Once I started questioning my desire to die, I became more aware of how others perceived my life. I started my working life as a stewardess with Singapore Airlines, and after six years, entered the advertising industry, including five years at Ogilvy & Mather, one of the world's leading agencies, followed by five years in corporate marketing at Four Seasons Hotels and Resorts. The privilege of working at the world's finest organisations was a source of pride for me. I was fortunate, and I knew it. On top of that, I was financially secure, by virtue of being married to my husband, a pilot with Singapore Airlines. I was living a charmed life. Yet, during all that time, I had spent too many days feeling an urge to end my life.

Feeling suicidal is simply having an urge to die. That irresistible urge in mental health patients is what doctors and academics tend to attribute to simple reasons, like hopelessness and desperation. For someone like me, with a mental health issue, whether medicated or not, I can find myself wanting to die simply because, at a given time, I find myself unable to cope with a random or particular situation. The source of such hopelessness can be difficult to identify. It could be one thing, or a combination of situations.

Thinking back to the times before my diagnosis, when I had seriously considered suicide, and what had led me to attempt suicide, I do not remember feeling particularly depressed. It was usually because I felt overwhelmed and helpless, unable to change my situation. This helplessness or self-loathing was brought on by one, or a combination, of a number of factors, for example, feeling the complete loss of control over my emotions, especially after ranting like a lunatic at my children for the slightest fault, which, in turn, left me feeling incapable of being a good parent. On such days, I would be convinced that my children deserved a better mother, and my husband needed a better wife. Interwoven with such convictions would be the belief that death had to be more attractive than life. I could never understand why I felt this way in the first place, seeing how comfortable my life was, but whenever I got this close to the edge, the feeling was always real, and the urge was always strong. It never occurred to me to question these feelings, because they did not last long – anything from about five minutes to two days.

It never took much to throw my mind into turmoil, followed immediately by fragility, when I felt like I was about to break into a million pieces. I would then crave peace and stillness, not just for that moment but forever. When the urge to die was so irresistible and so appealing, I became absolutely certain that death was the only way to escape from my mind and from myself. I would try to calm myself by reading or watching something on television, but it would be hard to focus. Occasionally, the urge lasted for more than a day, and that was when I would start planning my suicide: when I would die and how I would kill myself.

Then, within minutes, or hours, I would drop my plan, admonishing myself for over-reacting, and being dramatic. This about-turn would not necessarily be the result of a distraction; I have shut down thoughts of suicide simply from having changed my mind. Distractions have helped, though – like when a family member or friend says or does something which brings me a blast of immense joy; or when I look out of my balcony and see two hornbills flitting from tree to tree as if playing a game; or being forced to go out to commit to a lunch appointment with a close friend. These experiences have helped plans for suicide to disappear as quickly as they came.

Being in the presence of my family and a few close friends has helped to hold me back from attempting another suicide. The thought of them having to cope with my sudden and unexpected death, especially for my husband and children, who then have to pick up the pieces of life without a wife and a mother, has been enough to make me resolve to stay alive. Until the next time, and the next, and again and again, the cycle would always repeat itself. I swing from merely thinking about suicide and sometimes planning it, to finding a reason to live.

Considering the number of times I have thought about suicide, and planned it, and worse, going as far as attempting suicide, I have spent most of my life feeling non-suicidal. Which is to say, I have spent most of my life with all the appearances of a normal person – going to school, having a job, having friends, getting married, and raising children. But on days when I felt suicidal, even for just five minutes each day, three days in a row, the feeling was intense. I have spent most of my days feeling happy enough, but I rarely feel extremely thankful or joyful about being alive. On my low days, I know that as long as I stave off my urge to die, as long as I am alive, I will not cause pain to my family.

On suicidal days, I try as much as possible to focus on the consequences of my suicide to stay alive. Sometimes my mind can only process my own desperation, shutting out all reason. It is almost impossible to think rationally, and all I can think of is suicide. And then, I stop thinking about suicide, and decide to stay alive, telling myself to never go to that dark place again. Yet, inevitably, I do. Sometimes weeks later, sometimes months later. During the "circuit breaker" for the coronavirus pandemic, it was mere weeks in between. That's when I saw my doctor more often, who then added anti-psychotics to my medication regime.

The idea of suicide had begun to weave into and out of my head since I was in my teens, so whenever I found myself staring down from a height, wondering what it would be like to jump, it never felt unusual. But it was only in my early 30s when I found myself drawn to the brink of death. At that time, I was an account manager at Ogilvy & Mather. It was late at night, and I was exhausted after a week of working until nearly 10 o'clock every night. I had hardly seen my twins, who were three years old at that time. I was both angry with myself and sad for them, and as I walked to the multi-storey car park – I sometimes drove to work when my husband was away flying – I thought about how much I had failed them by not being around more often. They deserved better.

I put my bag in the car, and as if drawn like a moth to a flame, I deliberately walked straight ahead to the restraining wall and looked out, wondering what it would be like to jump eight floors down onto solid tarmac below with nothing to break my fall. I leaned forward slightly to try and get a better look at the ground below. Would my cold, lifeless body create a mess? Would my bones shatter and protrude from various parts? What if someone walked past just as I was about to hit the ground? I would kill that person, which would be murder, and worse, I may survive because he would have broken my fall. No, I thought, I would have to go somewhere without access to pedestrians. It did not occur to me that these were bad or wrong thoughts. They were merely thoughts. I felt very tired and wanted to sleep so I got into the car, turned up the music and headed home. Elmer Bernstein's *Magnificent Seven* had just started playing on the radio and, as it was used in the Marlboro commercials for a long time, it took me back to those carefree teenage days when my best friend and I were at the beach smoking and drinking when we were not supposed to. Five minutes of happy thoughts to a lively soundtrack made the drive home that much better. But those happy thoughts did not last very long.

A few days later, feeling too fatigued to even get dressed, I took two days off, my first sick leave after over a year at O&M. I slept most of the day, waking up in time to greet my kids at 3.30p.m., when they came home on the school bus. The next day, feeling too inadequate for needing sick leave just to rest and too morose to face my clients and colleagues, I drove to Toa Payoh in the early afternoon. I was familiar with Toa Payoh because I sometimes took my children to the library there. Also, Toa Payoh happened to be the closest HDB estate to my home. I parked the car near the library, walked to McDonald's and bought a strawberry sundae with extra topping. At that time, ice cream had been my comfort food of choice for more than 10 years. That day, I just felt like having an ice cream. I was not feeling particularly sad.

Holding the strawberry sundae in one hand, I crossed Toa Payoh Central. As I stood on the central divider, waiting for traffic on the other side to clear, my mind was blank, processing nothing, just watching the cars as they drove by. When I reached the block of flats on the other side of the road, I threw my now empty plastic sundae cup into the bin and took the lift up to the top floor. I don't remember feeling anything while waiting to reach the top floor. I looked below, just as I had done several times since I was a teenager. I was not feeling profoundly sad and I certainly was not despondent. I was not running away from a troubled life. I simply had this overwhelming urge to die that day and just as simply assumed it was normal. I do not remember for how long I stood at the staircase landing before deciding not to jump. I held back because at that very moment, I did not feel like dying.

As I sat in my car before driving off, I thought about how close I had come to ending my life just minutes ago. I thought about people like me and believed many people felt the same way about dying or changing their minds when finding themselves at the edge. They probably do not talk about their experience because some things are too embarrassing or stupid to discuss openly. Some people try to kill themselves and fail, while others succeed. Newspapers and television shows are never short of stories about people who killed themselves. It never crossed my mind that it was not normal to *want* to die. Especially when I had so much to live for.

Chapter 2

In all the years I spent in the advertising industry, I often found myself working with temperamental people, a disproportionate number of whom were in the creative department. It was almost as if a mercurial change in mood was a pre-requisite for creativity. But that was not true – I had worked with a few very talented creative people, and most of them were always calm. I, on the other hand, was erratic, but I was not in the creative department. I was in client servicing, where clients expected stability. Thankfully, in more than 10 years in advertising, I had mainly good clients, some who were remarkably clever and kind, which probably helped to keep me stable. I was aware of my temperament, but I never thought anything of it. If anything, I believed that I was perfectly suited for a career in the advertising industry. I certainly never thought my occasional outbursts were a problem requiring medical intervention.

One morning, while I was working at one of the advertising agencies, I had a meeting in my office with an account executive. We were going through our clients' budgets and allocations.

The monitor was moved towards her, so we could both view the screen at the same time. I made some revisions on an Excel file, explaining why as I went through the numbers. I noticed that she was staring blankly, with her hand under her chin. Concerned by her vague expression, I asked her if she knew how to use Excel. She looked at me, and with cheerful indifference, told me that it was not a problem, and that she would just use a calculator. The casual manner in which she excused herself from not doing something so basic, infuriated me.

I grabbed her wrist and glared at her while I screamed, asking if she was f**king retarded. She was silent, and I screamed at her again, asking the same question. I could sense the disquiet outside my office, and I could see through my window the executives and managers and secretaries all staring at their computers in hushed silence.

By now, I was trembling and realised that my behaviour was extreme and unacceptable. After a few seconds staring at the computer screen without actually seeing anything, I breathed deeply and, looked at this young woman in front of me. In stark contrast to my agitated state, she looked perfectly composed, and did not seem the least bit perturbed by my outburst. I apologised, but without meaning to sound defensive for a response that was indefensible, I reminded her that, as a 22-year-old, she should be teaching me to go beyond the basics in Excel. She smiled. I added that if she did not know something, then she had to take it upon herself to learn it. Telling me she would use the calculator did not take her back 10 years, it told me she was stupid and lazy. After a brief pause, I continued with the discussion as if nothing happened.

I had not experienced this rage in such a long time and had forgotten how quickly it came and went. Soon after, when the account executive had left the room, I leant back in my chair, shaken by what had just happened. I was extremely troubled by the utter lack of control as a person and a senior executive. I despaired at the aggression I had directed at this young woman, someone I was supposed to nurture. As in previous outbursts, I could not see this coming, nor could I control it, and this was exactly how it happened every single time. Except this episode shook me more than any other. So much so, I felt it necessary to confess my shameful behaviour to my family that night. I told my then 13-year-old twin daughters that if anyone ever spoke to them in that tone with such harsh words, they should just walk away, especially if it was at work. No job paid well enough to allow someone to humiliate another person like that which is what I had done to the poor girl that morning. I was fully aware that the greatest humiliation was brought upon myself. By the end of that evening, I knew I had to do something, but I did not know what.

A couple of weeks later, while speaking to a relative about the incident – I just could not seem to shake off just how I could so easily morph into such a reprehensible creature – she suggested I might be manic depressive. I had heard the term before, but did not know what it was. She explained that it was an illness characterised by mood swings. A mental illness. I was immediately defensive. How could I possibly be mad? She said that my father probably had the same illness; he was never diagnosed, but he had displayed all the classic symptoms. I was too upset to continue the conversation, but after I ended the call, I sank into the sofa, stared at the ceiling and thought of my late father, wondering if there was any truth to what I had just heard. I thought about some of the things he had said and done, and my mother's exasperation and fear. Perhaps I was a little like him; I was, after all, his daughter. But surely all that we did was not enough to make us manic depressive? Desperate to understand what this term really meant, I searched the Internet, which offered enough information for me to spend the rest of the morning pondering what I had read. I decided I had to see a doctor.

Early the next week, I postponed a client meeting and went to see a psychiatrist recommended by our family doctor. He had a kindly demeanour and grey hair which made me feel I was in the hands of an experienced doctor. He asked me many questions, most of them very personal. He stressed that answers had to be honest and qualified with examples, and explained that unlike most major illnesses, mental disorders could not be diagnosed with blood tests and brain scans. My answers would be used to evaluate my symptoms based on the detailed criteria in *Diagnostic and Statistical Manual for Mental Disorders*, that widely respected diagnostic tool used by psychiatrists worldwide.

Even though I had read some of the questions doctors usually ask during a patient's first visit, I was not prepared for my reaction. Several times, I stood up, ready to walk out, but was told that if I wanted help, I needed to co-operate. Many of the questions were too personal and intrusive. Do you often feel extremely energetic? Do you have a very active sex life? Have you been promiscuous? Are you an impulsive person? Are you involved in a goal-directed activity? How many hours of sleep do you need? Tell me about the last time you lost your temper and what caused it. Are you very talkative, speaking very quickly? What about times when you've been very sad, have you experienced that before? Do people have trouble keeping up with you? How much caffeine do you consume a day? Do you crave sugar or sweet things like cake and ice cream? Do you shop impulsively, buying things you do not need or many quantities of the same items? Tell me your plans for the future. Do you have a family history of mental illness? Alcohol or substance abuse? Suicidal ideation[1] was discussed, more extensively than all the other symptoms, and evaluated for the diagnosis.

After almost two hours of questioning, I was diagnosed with Bipolar Disorder Type 1, the classic and most severe form of the illness. According to the doctor, I had experienced several manic episodes. It took some time for the doctor's words to sink in and once it did, I was shattered to realise that the diagnosis meant I was now a mental patient, and that I was simply, for want of a better word, mad. I was 42 years old.

As I was about to leave, I suggested to the doctor that my behaviour might be because I am an extreme person, and unusually expressive. Some people are like that, and not necessarily mentally ill. The doctor smiled kindly and agreed that I might just be an extreme person. But I had clearly established a pattern of extreme behaviour as evidenced by the presence and duration of my signs and symptoms and those were the biggest tell-tale signs, the pattern of my mood swings from mania to depression. He assured me his diagnosis was

---

1   Suicidal ideation, also known as suicidal thoughts, is when a person thinks about, considers, or plans a suicide. It is a symptom of some mental disorders. Passive suicidal ideation is thinking about not wanting to live or imagining being dead. Active suicidal ideation is planning how to kill oneself.

accurate, and assured me that medication and therapy would help me be more balanced.

I was still having trouble accepting the fact that I now had a label to live with. I looked at him and rattled off the questions. Don't most people at some point have mood swings, happy today and sad tomorrow or even the same day? Don't many people shop impulsively? Surely it isn't the bipolar world keeping retail alive? Don't a lot of people get by on too little sleep? By the time he had answered the first two questions, we had lost track of the questions. The doctor then went on to explain the importance of taking the medication diligently, in the right dosage, at the right time. Just before I left his room, he explained that bipolar is multi-dimensional, and my most basic level mood swings often took me from increased self-esteem to feeling worthless, from being excessively happy to intensely sad.

I was given several packets of medication, one of which was labelled "anti-psychotic", and a medical certificate exempting me from work for several days. I called my husband from the car park and told him what the doctor had said. We agreed we had to tell our children, twin girls who were 14 years old at that time. Over dinner, I told them I had bipolar disorder and explained what it was. They seemed sympathetic and understanding, especially when I apologised for the many outbursts they had suffered over the years. As a close family, we decided to assign the blame to my illness rather than to me, and looked forward with relief to years ahead of stability from medication.

In my desperation to get well, I promised myself that I would be diligent with my medication and started taking them that very night. The doctor did not tell me anything about the medication he was prescribing and did not bother to tell me about the side effects. As I was in a daze just trying to process the diagnosis, it never occurred to me to ask him.

I woke up the next morning feeling hungover. I no longer remember how the next few days passed but I do remember feeling numb most of the time. I did not have an episode, neither manic nor depressive. I did not have an urge to die, probably because the medication made me feel dead anyway. I could not bear to be at home, with the children in school and my husband away. A few days after seeing the doctor, I returned to work while still on medical leave. The life that had felt sucked out of me in the days before returned as soon as I put on my work clothes, some jewellery, my favourite perfume, and a heavy application of my signature traffic-stopping red lipstick. The environment in an advertising agency is lively at most times so it helped to be in the office, engaging with colleagues, and my wonderful team of account executives. That evening, I resolved not to be a zombie, and to find a way to heal myself without medication. I threw away two of the three packets of medication, keeping only the sleeping pills, expecting to use them on some weekends when I needed to catch up on sleep.

The next day, I cancelled the follow-up appointment with the psychiatrist. I decided that I was not mentally ill and I was going to be fine.

Chapter 3

Previously known as manic depressive illness, bipolar disorder is a psychiatric condition characterised by mood swings from extreme lows to extreme highs. In a booklet published by Singapore's Ministry of Health in 2011, bipolar disorder is described as a "chronic relapsing illness, and if left untreated, may pose significant morbidity and suicide risks."

According to a study published in 2017,[1] the share of mental disorders amongst the global population was estimated at nearly 11%. That means, nearly 800 million people around the world were estimated to have a mental disorder, which includes the following (in order of prevalence): depression, anxiety, bipolar disorder, eating disorders (clinical anorexia and bulimia), and schizophrenia. For bipolar disorder, the global prevalence was 0.6% or 46 million people worldwide, nearly eight times the total population of Singapore.

The Singapore Mental Health Study 2016 was a comprehensive national psychiatric epidemiological study among adults in Singapore led by the Institute of Mental Health in collaboration with the Ministry of Health, Nanyang Technological University

---

1   *Institute for Health Metrics and Evaluation* and reported in their flagship Global Burden of Disease study.

and Saw Swee Hock School of Public Health. According to this study, one in seven people in Singapore has experienced a mental disorder. Major depressive disorder was highest at 6.3%, followed by alcohol abuse (4.1%), obsessive compulsive disorder (3.6%), bipolar disorder (1.6%) and schizophrenia (1%). For any of the above illnesses, the prevalence was 13.9%.

The International Classification of Diseases from the World Health Organisation[2] and the *Diagnostic and Statistical Manual*[3] from the American Psychiatric Association are the two main schemes for diagnosing bipolar disorder. Both these schemes are quite similar; doctors in Singapore use the *Diagnostic and Statistical Manual* (DSM) which differentiates between bipolar I and bipolar II disorders. The current DSM is the fifth edition, known as DSM-V. Being full of heavily researched information covering symptoms, descriptions and criteria, it is favoured by doctors and hospitals all over the world to diagnose mental disorders in patients.

These two mood extremes of bipolar disorder– the lowest low (melancholia or depression) and the highest high (mania) – were first documented by the ancient Greek physician, Hippocrates of Kos (460–337 BCE). Widely regarded as the Father of Medicine, Hippocrates worked to define this mental disorder as being separate from temperament. A few hundred years later, Aretaeus of Cappadocia (2 AD), another ancient Greek physician, emphasised the biological origin of melancholia, which differed from the psychological reaction termed "reactive depression". Both Hippocrates and Aretaeus believed that mania and melancholia as expressed by the patients they studied

2   10th edition ICD-10

3   4th edition text revised DSM-IV TR

were neither innate personality traits, nor were they reactions to specific situations. It was Aretaeus who first made the link between the two extreme states of mind, mania and melancholia, and created a spectrum within these extremes. He believed that melancholia and mania were the same condition and stemmed from a dysfunction of the brain. Nearly 2,000 years later, during the mid-19th century, Aretaeus' concept of mania and melancholia was re-examined by a few respected psychiatrists in France and Germany. In 1980, with the publication of DSM-III, the word bipolar disorder was used for the first time to describe manic depressive insanity.[4]

When I was diagnosed with bipolar disorder in 2005, the doctor had used DSM-IV (1994) for the diagnosis. The criteria were very similar to DSM-III (1980), where certain symptoms were highlighted.[5]

Elevated mood is described as "euphoric, unusually good, cheerful or high; often has an infectious quality for the uninvolved observer; but was recognized as excessive by those who know the individual well" and is considered the "prototypical symptom", mentioning that irritability may be present or the predominant mood symptom, likely when the individual is "thwarted".

Overtalkativeness was explained as "manic speech, typically loud, rapid, and difficult to interrupt".

Flight of ideas was described as a "nearly continuous flow of accelerated speech with abrupt changes from topic to topic".

Hyperactivity encompasses increased activity in numerous social domains and "often involves excessive planning of and participation in multiple activities... almost invariably there is

4   The National Center for Biotechnology Information
5   American Psychiatric Association, DSM-III

increased sociability... the intrusive, domineering, and demanding nature of these interactions is not recognized by the individual", but the lack of need for sleep was specifically mentioned, "awakens several hours before usual time, full of energy... may go days without any sleep at all and yet not feel tired". "Frequently, expansiveness, unwarranted optimism, grandiosity, and lack of judgement lead to such activities as buying sprees... have a disorganized, flamboyant, or bizarre quality".

All of the above symptoms described me with a good measure of accuracy – my behaviour and my mind, at one point or another, starting in my teens. The questions the doctor had asked during that first visit were obviously crafted for the above criteria, allowing a diagnosis to be made, and for medication to be prescribed.

For the next few months after my diagnosis, followed swiftly by dumping my pills, I felt alright. I felt sociable and energetic again. I did not think I was particularly manic, and I did not feel depressive. One day, my boss called me in to his office to say that a few colleagues had mentioned – a euphemism for complained – to him about my "exuberance". He had paused before saying the word. I thought it was a good thing, bringing energy and cheerfulness to the office. But that was not how my colleagues saw my behaviour. They were concerned at best, and some were even exasperated. I told my boss that I had been diagnosed with bipolar disorder and that I had stopped taking my medication because of the side effects. He was very kind and understanding and suggested I seek help. It was a wake-up call to acknowledge my illness and take it seriously.

That weekend, I saw my family doctor and asked him if he could recommend a good psychiatrist. I told him that I was not comfortable with the previous psychiatrist, but could not explain why other than being upset with not being told anything about the mind-altering medication. He then recommended me to a well-known psychiatrist in private practice.

The next psychiatrist I saw diagnosed me similarly as having Type 1 bipolar disorder. I was not surprised, but as I had hoped for better news, I was devastated at the same time. This confirmed that I was, without doubt, mad. In other words commonly used in Singapore, I was *xiao, gila*. As the words sank in, I felt deeply ashamed of myself and resolved to get better. This time, I promised myself that I would stay on my medication and make myself well. The new prescription comprised a cocktail of three drugs to be taken at various times, the most potent being the sedative which I had to take every night. I took the medication exactly as prescribed. The side effects in the first week were difficult to deal with and as much as I was tempted to throw them away like I had done before, I persevered. On any given day, I felt at least two of the following: sleepiness, nausea, dry mouth, chills, weakness, restlessness and dizziness. I also had nightmares, stomach cramps, and my head hurt. Clumsiness and weakness in my limbs were the most noticeable and distressful side effects especially during lunch at a food court, when I had to carry a tray with a bowl of boiling hot noodle soup and a drink. I also felt weepy, got tired easily and had to suck on mints constantly just to take away the dryness in my mouth. The doctor assured me these were common side effects and advised me to give it time.

For weeks, I was too subdued and missed my old self. Back in those days, even at my worst, when I was listless, I knew I would bounce back in no time. Right now, I did not know if this was the new me. It was taking too long to feel better, to feel 'normal'. I felt I could no longer control my mind. I did not like, nor even recognise, the person I had become. I could not and did not want to wait. Now, more than ever, I wanted to die.

Chapter 4

For all the times over the years that I had thought about taking my own life before my diagnosis in 2005, I had only ever flirted with death – going to the very edge to kill myself – a few times before walking away.

In late 2005, towards the end of a particularly challenging week at work, while at the same time struggling to cope with the side effects of medication, the urge to die weaved its way in and out of my head with frightening regularity and intensity. By the end of that Friday afternoon, I could barely focus and left the office at five o'clock and drove to meet my children at the club where they were having their riding lessons. They were surprised and happy to see me. After their lesson, we went home and had a special dinner. We had champagne which I poured into three exquisite champagne glasses. My husband and I collected champagne glasses and we had about 12 different ones. I let them choose their glass. One of my daughters asked what we were celebrating, as she held a handmade, etched glass with just enough champagne for two or three sips. Life, I answered, we are celebrating life. The other daughter asked what it was about life that we were celebrating. I was not expecting a question like that and did not know how to answer it. Just life, I said, smiling at them, thinking how lovely they were.

Soon after they had gone to bed, I wrote a few very personal words on patterned stationery for my husband and children. When I started to write, I had found myself unable to explain the need to take such a drastic step, something that would impact their lives for a very long time. I was running out of time to think so I simply told them how much I adored them and that bad things were happening inside my head and I did not know what else to do or where else to go. I begged them to forgive me.

I then wrote a few more notes to close friends and three or four colleagues who were particularly kind to me, including my boss, followed by an email about my illness and having to go away. I had chosen a euphemism to avoid alarming anyone who might scuttle my plan. With just one press of a button, nearly one hundred and fifty people all over the world received this email.

It was now 9.30 at night, and my husband was due home at around 11.30, maybe 11.15 if he landed early. I had just two hours to do everything I needed to. I switched off the computer before any responses came in and called my mother who was living in California at that time. She was not on the email list. I told her I was not well and she said she would pray for me. We spoke for 15 minutes about her health and her friends. When the call ended, I left the phone off the hook.

I went to the kitchen, took the bottle of leftover champagne, the little packet of sleeping pills from the first doctor I had seen, a stiff and waxy plastic carrier bag from Marks & Spencer, a roll of thick packing tape and a box cutter. I went to the guest room and shut the door. The lock didn't work so I pushed a table against the door. I drank a glass of champagne and looked at the time. It was just before 10 o'clock. I was ready for a deep and sound sleep and not make a mess. I did not, could not, think about anything else.

I had another glass of champagne and took eight pills, all that were left from the ten I had been given previously. I finished the second glass of champagne and slid the carrier bag over my head. I had specifically chosen the Marks & Spencer one because it was the perfect size and being made from a stiff and waxy plastic, it would be impossible for me to tear it off with my stubby fingers if I panicked and changed my mind at the last minute. This important detail only occurred to me when I was rummaging in the storeroom for an appropriate bag. I then ran the packing tape – soft plastic which was easy to twirl around and wide enough to cover large areas – across my face and under my chin and ensured every bit was tightly sealed. Before I could finish, I could feel the deepest sleep creeping up on me, slowly but surely. As I cut the tape, I thought about also slashing my wrists, just to be sure, but it had seemed too violent and would have been messy. I was also afraid of the pain from a deep gash. I put the cutter away and lay down to sleep on the floor. I instinctively looked at my watch but could not see through the translucent bag. I could not tell how many minutes had passed. I knew that I would be asleep in a few minutes and suffocate in 15 minutes, 30 tops, with the life sucked completely out of me long before my husband got home.

I felt happy and calm and completely at peace. I thought about my beloved late Amah, smiling at me, as she had been doing from the photograph which I had been carrying in my wallet for more than 20 years. She had been more than a nanny to me and I looked forward to seeing her again. A moment later, I felt nothing. I must have fallen asleep and as far as I knew, just before then, I was not going to wake up again. For decades I had thought of death, my own death on my own terms. And now, it was happening.

I was finally ready to die.

But I did not die that night. Instead, I woke up in the hospital. I was seen by a rather brusque doctor, who asked me some questions, before being admitted to a ward. I had no idea what time it was. My head ached and all I wanted to do was sleep.

My husband stayed by my side while the nurse made arrangements for me to be warded at Tan Tock Seng Hospital. My husband sat at the edge of my bed, looking worn and much older than when he had left for Beijing two days before. His eyes were soft and gentle, as I had always known them to be. He did not seem angry. I wanted to know what happened, but at that moment, feeling like a failure, I was too ashamed to ask what had happened. He deserved answers more than I did.

I told him that I had felt like dying for a very long time. I could not explain why, but the feeling was always there, circling in my head. It had always felt normal to me, and tonight seemed to be the right time. I hated what was going on inside my head, that feeling of not being in control, of being unpredictable and helpless and not knowing when my demons would strike.

It was now my turn to ask what had happened, why was I not dead?

My husband explained how he had arrived home much earlier than expected. How was that possible, on a seven-hour flight?

The winds were in his favour, which shaved nearly 30 minutes off his flight time, and, when he arrived at Changi, he had breezed through the process of submitting his reports because he had not had a trainee to debrief. By landing earlier, he did not get crew transport, which sometimes meant a long wait for the co-ordinator to arrange a taxi. Instead, he walked straight to the taxi rank, where he was first in line for a taxi. By now, he was almost 40 minutes earlier from when he was due home. As traffic on the Pan Island Expressway was light, the taxi driver decided that he would significantly increase his speed. My husband was home in 20 minutes. All in, he managed to be home an hour earlier. When he found me, I was barely alive. And now, here we were – me, pulled against my wishes from the brink of death by a husband who was struggling to understand why.

Before he left the room, my husband made me promise never to even contemplate suicide again. I promised, with every intention of keeping it. It was, and still remains, a difficult promise to keep. But I do try, and sometimes I try very, very hard.

Chapter 5

Every day, somewhere around the world, people kill themselves. Not everyone writes a suicide note. For the millions[1] who have killed themselves over the centuries, there are no statistics on suicide notes. Does the incidence on note-writing vary by ethnic groups? Or gender? Age, perhaps? Do children or teenagers ever leave behind a note? Having written several notes the night I had tried to kill myself, I was curious, and disappointed not to be able to find any useful information.

In the 1960s and 1970s, a number of doctors and researchers who wanted to understand the mystery around suicide began studying suicide notes, believing they would provide insights into the suicidal mind. However, results of such studies proved to be inconclusive, reflecting scientific analysis more than what leads a person to the path of self-annihilation.

While I cannot remember the contents of the notes I had written for various people, I can remember to whom I had written. It was less than an hour before my attempt when I had written the personal note cards and an email which was broadcast to everyone on my yahoo email list. My mind would

---

1 According to Global Burden of Disease Study 2017, deaths from suicide between 1990 and 2016 have ranged between 750,000 and 830,000, peaking at 860,000 in 1995. In 16 years alone, at least 10 million lives were lost to suicide.

have been in turmoil, yet I remember approaching the writing in a cold, methodical way, as if sending a message that needed to be understood with absolute clarity. None of my notes would have been of much use to researchers, but, had I died that night, I would have liked my notes to have helped my family and friends understand my anguish.

In a study conducted by Dr. Edwin S. Shneidman[2] (1918–2009), a pre-eminent psychologist and suicidologist, who had dedicated his life to studying suicide and founded America's first comprehensive suicide prevention centre, a suicide note is an essential source for a view into a suicidal mind. Together with fellow psychologist Norman Farberow (1918–2015), Shneidman embarked on studying suicide notes, the most instructive of which were the five suicide notes of a woman named Natalie, a subject in the Genetic Studies of Genius, now known as the Terman Study of the Gifted.[3] Although the study was conducted in 1957, these suicides notes remain Shneidman's best-known case study.

As I read Natalie's notes, I was struck by a familiarity, as if I might have written some of them. Excluding the references to her ex-husband, the letters to her friend and her daughters resonated with me. After reading all five notes, I tried to imagine if I really might have expressed similar sentiments. I asked myself, was it possible that a mind so anguished to the extent of being about to execute a permanent exit, could write with such clarity

2   Dr. Edwin Shneidman was the chief of America's first national suicide prevention programme at the National Institute of Mental Health; founded the American Association of Suicidology and America's first comprehensive suicide prevention centre; and was the first professor of thanatology (the study of death) at the University of California, Los Angeles. Due to his extensive research and the publication of countless academic papers and over 20 books, Dr. Shneidman is credited with raising awareness for suicide starting in the late 1950s. By establishing the study of suicide as an interdisciplinary field in psychology, Dr. Shneidman introduced concepts which are now widely practised by psychologists and doctors worldwide.

3   According to Shneidman's archives from the 1950s, there are extremely high rates of suicide among gifted people.

and precision? Yes, I believe it is possible if, in the event of a successful suicide, it was essential to assuage the guilt of loved ones left behind, especially those who might blame themselves or ask what they could have done to prevent the death, and also for providing specific instructions that need to be fulfilled. Both reasons for a suicide note were covered in Natalie's five notes, which, throughout showed how desperate she was to die. Not everyone has the ability to write as eloquently as Natalie – she was a genius, after all – but it must be harder for a person writing a farewell note in the hours or days before dying. Suicide notes vary from a few words to a 1,900-page tome written by a young man who shot himself. As Shneidman found, very few notes express the anguish of a suicidal mind, while giving clear instructions what those left behind must do.

Natalie wrote:[4]

1. To her adult friend: *Rosalyn – Get Eastern Steel Co. – Tell them and they will find Bob right away. Papa is at his business. Betty is at the Smiths – Would you ask Helene to keep her until her Daddy comes – so she won't know until he comes for her. You have been so good – I love you – Please keep in touch with Betty – Natalie.*

2. To her eldest daughter: *Betty, go over to Rosalyn's right away – Get in touch with Papa.*

3. To her ex-husband, from whom she was recently divorced: *Bob, – I'm making all kinds of mistakes with our girls – They have to have a leader and every day the job seems more enormous – You couldn't have been a better Daddy to Nancy and they do love you – Nancy misses you so and she doesn't*

---

4   *Suicide as Psychache: A Clinical Approach to Self-destructive Behavior,* Edwin S Shneidman, Jason Aronson Inc, 1995.

know what's the matter – I know you've built a whole new life for yourself but make room for the girls and keep them with you – Take them where you go – It's only for just a few years – Betty is almost ready to stand on her own two feet – But Nancy needs you desperately. Nancy needs help – She really thinks you didn't love her – and she's got to be made to do her part for her own self-respect – Nancy hasn't been hurt much yet – but ah! the future if they keep on the way I've been going lately – Barbara sounds warm and friendly and relaxed and I pray to God she will understand just a little and be good to my girls – they need two happy people – not a sick mixed-up mother – There will be a little money to help with extras – It had better go that way than for more pills and more doctor bills – I wish to God it had been different but be happy – but please – stay by your girls – And just one thing – be kind to Papa (his father) – He's done everything he could to try to help me – He loves the girls dearly and it's right that they should see him often – Natalie Bob – this afternoon Betty and Nancy had such a horrible fight it scares me. Do you suppose Gladys and Orville would take Betty for this school year? She should be away from Nancy for a little while – in a calm atmosphere.

4. To her husband's father: *Papa – no one could have been more kind or generous than you have been to me – I know you couldn't understand this – and forgive me – The lawyer had copy of my will – Everything equal – the few personal things I have of value – the bracelet to Nancy and my wedding ring to Betty – But I would like Betty to have Nana's diamond – have them appraised and give Betty and Nancy each half of the diamonds in the band. Please have somebody come in and*

clean – Have Bob take the girls away immediately – I don't want them to have to stay around – You're so good Papa dear.

5.   To her two children: *My dearest ones – You two have been the most wonderful things in my life – Try to forgive me for what I've done – your father would be so much better for you. It will be harder for you for a while – but so much easier in the long run – I'm getting you all mixed up – Respect and love are almost the same – Remember that – and the most important thing is to respect yourself – The only way you can do that is by doing your share and learning to stand on your own two feet – Betty try to remember the happy times – and be good to Nancy. Promise me you will look after your sister's welfare – I love you very much – but I can't face what the future will bring.*

Natalie makes clear her distress – *I can't face what the future will bring* – and her belief that her death will be better for her children – *so much easier in the long run*. Even in that state of mind, having made the decision to kill herself, and going on to write heartfelt notes to people closest to her, Natalie was able to give precise instructions to her friend, her ex-husband and his father, and to her children. She also expressed her love for her children and asked for forgiveness. She then swallowed an unknown amount of prescription pills, lay on her bedroom floor while resting her head on a pillow, and died, presumably a while later.

In celebrity suicides without an accompanying note, media speculation is rife, and the spotlight on the family is harsh and thoughtless. When a note is found, the reporting tends to be less intense, with reporters not trying to outdo each other to find out the "real reason" for the suicide. As in the high-profile suicides of celebrity chef, writer and travel journalist Anthony Bourdain, and fashion designer and entrepreneur Kate Spade, speculation continues long after their suicides.

Having read a number of notes from high-profile suicides believed to have been contributed by bipolar disorder (or manic depressive illness, as it was known before the 1980s), and having written several myself, it is quite fascinating how such notes can be written so calmly, with such rational thought, only to haunt a reader long after. I have included here a small selection of suicide notes, of which I have found the most poignant letter to be the one Virginia Woolf, one of the most influential writers of the 20th century, wrote to her husband, Leonard, in March 1941, before filling her coat pockets with rocks, walking into the River Ouse near her home in England, and drowning herself:

Dearest,

I feel certain I am going mad again. I feel we can't go through another of those terrible times. And I shan't recover this time. I begin to hear voices, and I can't concentrate. So I am doing what seems the best thing to do. You have given me the greatest possible happiness. You have been in every way all that anyone could be. I don't think two people could have been happier till this terrible disease came. I can't fight any longer. I know that I am spoiling your life, that without me you could work. And you will I know. You see I can't even write this properly. I can't read. What I want to say is I owe all the happiness of my life to you. You have been entirely patient with me and incredibly good. I want to say that – everybody knows it. If anybody could have saved me it would

*have been you. Everything has gone from me but the certainty
of your goodness. I can't go on spoiling your life any longer.
I don't think two people could have been happier than we
have been.*

If ever I had to write another suicide note – and I can only
hope that I never get to that point ever again – I would glad to be
able to express my sentiments with a fraction of such eloquence.
If I had to resort to plagiarism, I would borrow these lines in the
notes that I would – but hope not to – write to my husband and
daughters: "*What I want to say is I owe all the happiness of my life
to you. You have been entirely patient with me and incredibly good.
I want to say that – everybody knows it.*"

In April 1994, Kurt Cobain, the lead singer and guitarist of
the most successful rock band of the '90s, was found dead in his
home in Seattle, Washington. His suicide note was addressed to
Boddah, his imaginary friend, but towards the end, he addresses
his wife and refers to his young daughter. Cobain was only 27
years old, with wealth estimated at US$150 million and at the
peak of his popularity when he pulled the trigger and blasted
his head with his shotgun. Handwritten in red ink, Cobain's
two-page suicide note is largely about his disenchantment with
stardom:

*For example, when we're back stage and the lights go out
and the manic roar of the crowds begins, it doesn't affect me
the way in which it did for Freddie Mercury, who seemed to
love, relish in the love and adoration from the crowd which*

is something I totally admire and envy. The fact is, I can't fool you, any one of you. It simply isn't fair to you or me. The worst crime I can think of would be to rip people off by faking it and pretending as if I'm having 100% fun. Sometimes I feel as if I should have a punch-in time clock before I walk out on stage. I've tried everything within my power to appreciate it (and I do, God, believe me, I do, but it's not enough). I appreciate the fact that I and we have affected and entertained a lot of people. It must be one of those narcissists who only appreciate things when they're gone. I'm too sensitive. I need to be slightly numb in order to regain the enthusiasms I once had as a child.

The last few words from one of the greatest musicians in the history of rock music show the sheer anguish he must have lived through while his band was reaching for the stars, and grabbing a few along the way.

Thank you all from the pit of my burning, nauseous stomach for your letters and concern during the past years. I'm too much of an erratic, moody baby! I don't have the passion anymore, and so remember, it's better to burn out than to fade away.[5]

Peace, love, empathy.
Kurt Cobain

---

5   "It's better to burn out than to fade away" is a line from the song 'My, My, Hey, Hey Out of the Blue' (1978) by singer songwriter Neil Young. For a while after Cobain's death, this line became a popular expression for teen angst worldwide.

Frances and Courtney, I'll be at your altar. Please keep going Courtney, for Frances. For her life, which will be so much happier without me. I LOVE YOU, I LOVE YOU!"

And then he shot himself.

After his suicide note was made public, there was much discussion about how anyone who claimed to love his daughter that much, could then abandon her in such a violent suicide. I would have asked the same, had I read his suicide note at the time. I now know that it is a most difficult thing to do, to commit suicide and leave behind people we love to pick up the pieces.

Woolf said, "*I can't fight any longer. I know that I am spoiling your life, that without me you could work. And you will I know.*" Cobain said, "*For her life, which will be so much happier without me.*" Different words, similar sentiment, as have been found in countless suicide notes, all expressing great love for the people left behind, and a belief that their deaths will improve the lives of their loved ones. Much like I had done when I had written to my husband and daughters that night. Except that I did not die; I was pulled away just as I had brushed my fingers against the gates of hell.

Chapter 6

As was typical in agency life, I worked long hours. I enjoyed my job – I was then working at my first advertising agency, a medium-sized international agency headquartered in New York; I had colleagues who were friendly, helpful and good-humoured; and I worked with an inspiring boss who taught me more than I needed to know to survive in an industry notorious for being competitive and unforgiving. I had a small circle of good friends. Financially, we were comfortable enough. In short, I could not have asked for more.

Yet, I thought of suicide often. On my best days, the thoughts were non-existent. On many days, they were fleeting. On my worst days, the thoughts morphed into an obsession where I sometimes ventured into an extremely dark crevice in my mind and began to plan my exit. Years later, after I was diagnosed with bipolar disorder, and had learnt more about my mind, I would sometimes look back and think about the times I went so far as to plan my suicide, without carrying it out. With the diagnosis, and the information I had about the illness, it made sense that I had found suicide to be an appealing escape.

Now, nearly 30 years later, my suicidal ideation has been largely stable, except in 2020, when passive suicidal ideation was the norm for at least a few days a week, and active suicidal ideation happened a few times a month, depending on situations. On such days, when something would happen, I would be overwhelmed, like when I was writing a novel with my husband, and, because he used a very different process in his writing, I was unable to adapt, and would feel like I was drowning, unable to cope. Most times, passive suicidal ideation kicked in, but there were two instances when passive suicidal ideation rapidly became active suicidal ideation, and, fighting the urge before it took hold of my mind, I immediately stopped writing, shut my laptop and did something mindless, like scrolling through social media on my phone.

It has never taken much for me to feel that my mind just cannot cope with the situation at hand and that my only escape is death. Yet, for most people, such situations are easily managed without much thought. I tell myself what I often hear others saying – get on with it. But I cannot just "get on with it"; I simply do not know how to, nor do I have the will. It is as if my mind has shut down, and needs to stop functioning.

Several years after my diagnosis, when I first connected the two emotions – feeling overwhelmed and the urge to die – I asked myself if I had become extremely weak or stupid over the years. I was sure that many of my good brain cells had been vaporised by the psychiatric medication I had been on. By then I was a patient at IMH, and every time I saw my doctor, I gave him examples of situations which had me feeling as if I was carrying such a heavy load, that I could not even take another step. As I did not want to be warded or heavily medicated for suicidal ideation, or worse, be put through electroconvulsive therapy,[1] I would avoid saying anything about wanting to die. Instead, I would tell him that, in such instances, I just wanted to run away and hide but had nowhere to go. He assured me that I was not stupid. He said that I was a perfectionist and should try not to focus on the little things, and that I should try to lower my expectations and accept that things did not always have to be a certain way. Yes, you're right, I would say, agreeing each time, genuinely believing I would heed his advice and apply it the moment I walked out of his room. By the time I reached home, I realised I could not be the person the doctor suggested I try being.

---

1   Also known as ECT or shock therapy, this is a procedure done under general anaesthesia. Small electric currents are sent through the brain, to trigger a brief seizure. The resulting changes in brain chemistry is known to reverse symptoms of certain mental conditions including suicide.

Chapter 7

When someone with a high profile commits suicide, especially a celebrity, the media is quick to report the death, along with speculation and interviews with anyone who can claim even the most remote connection to the celebrity. In this age of social media, millions feel at liberty to add to the story, with tributes overflowing in countless languages across the internet.

In 2019, two popular celebrities killed themselves within a week of each other. On June 5, 2018, Katherine Noel Valentine Brosnahan Spade, known as Kate Spade, founder of the wildly popular brand of handbags and accessories, was found hanged in her Manhattan apartment. The next day, her husband, Andy Spade, issued a statement:

"Kate suffered from depression and anxiety for many years. She was actively seeking help and working closely with doctors to treat her disease, one that takes far too many lives. We were in touch with her the night before and she sounded happy. There was no indication and no warning that she would do this. It was a complete shock. And it clearly wasn't her. There were personal demons she was battling."

The condolences poured in. People struggled to understand how a woman who created such whimsical, cheerful bags, clothes, shoes and accessories could be battling demons, only to give up and kill herself. I did not participate in any of the conversations on social media, but every time something appeared on my news feed, I felt sad. Kate Spade was only two months younger than me, and she had suffered from disorders which had also plagued me for decades. Her suicide took me back to when I had made my first attempt. I thought about all those times, years before, when I had thought about taking my own life. Several times I had gone beyond merely thinking about suicide; I had even planned it. When was the first time and how many times had Kate Spade thought about suicide before she hanged herself? On the day her suicide made the news, I pulled out a gorgeous card wallet a very dear friend had given me one Christmas. I had used it for a while, and had then put it away to extend its lifespan. I have used the card wallet for my bus card and a debit card ever since.

Three days later, just as social media was beginning to wean itself off Kate Spade's suicide, another celebrity death shocked the world. Celebrity chef Anthony Michael Bourdain was found hanged in his hotel room in France. Once again, the internet world was plastered with messages of sympathy. It was worse, I think, because people were also referring to Kate Spade's death just days before. Unlike Kate Spade's death, where "anxiety" and "depression" were mentioned, there was nothing said about Anthony Bourdain's state of mind.

Bourdain's suicide hit me harder than any celebrity suicide I could think of. After years of watching his shows, I felt like I had lost someone I had adored and known quite well. But my absolute adoration of him started long before I watched him on television. Sometime in the early 2000s, Anthony Bourdain was the star of an event at the Four Seasons Hotel, co-hosted by his friend and Singapore's premier street-food consultant, K.F. Seetoh. My friends and I had a table for 10 at the back of the room. During a question-and-answer session, someone in the audience asked Bourdain what he thought about chicken rice. He paused before sheepishly answering, *I have not tried that yet.* I immediately shouted out a loud, *Boo!* Just once, but it was immediately followed by a number of boos from the audience. It lasted a few seconds, and the audience went silent as soon as Bourdain spoke. He said he was going to have some chicken rice with Seetoh within the next few days. After the talk and when most of us had finished our meal, Bourdain went from table to table to say hello. When he came to our table, I apologised profusely for initiating the booing, and Bourdain, in turn, apologised for not making it a priority to try Singapore's national dish. Both Bourdain and Seetoh sat at our table and the rest of us enjoyed some lively conversation with these two most amiable gentlemen. This memory of him exacerbated the horror of his tragic death.

Why did Anthony Bourdain kill himself? Did he have a mental disorder of some sort, like Kate Spade? I searched the news for days after that, and found that in his book, *Kitchen Confidential*, Bourdain had spoken candidly about his depression and substance abuse. A line from his book resonated with me, starting with my six years of working as a stewardess in Singapore Airlines through to my five years at the Asia Pacific headquarters of Four Seasons Hotels and Resorts and thereafter, to other places at which I had worked:

> *"I was in hiding, in a deep, dark hole, and it was dawning on me – as I cracked my oysters, and opened clams, and spooned cocktail sauce into ramekins – that it was time, really time, to try to climb out."*

And climb out he certainly did. Bourdain had climbed up and up, going from hot-shot chef to bestselling author and, just before he died, uber-popular television host. He had been open about his struggles with depression, and also talked about his abysmal lows, while travelling the world sampling exotic dishes, all the while presenting a most affable persona on what must have been gruelling shoots for his various culinary-travel programmes. It was on one of these shoots that Bourdain hanged himself in his hotel room in France, without leaving any clue as to what might have led him to hang himself in the middle of filming a very popular series, *Parts Unknown*, with people he knew, doing a job he loved. He was 61 years old, and immensely successful. According to reports, Bourdain had dined with Eric Ripert, his best friend, and one of the world's greatest chefs, at Michelin-starred Auberge de l'Ill two nights before his death. The sommelier at the restaurant was reported as saying that the three of them had a lively exchange about wine and food pairings, and that they seemed happy. The night before he killed himself, he had not shown up for dinner with Ripert. The next morning, after Ripert had waited for quite some time and there was still no sign of Bourdain at breakfast, Ripert went to check on Bourdain with a receptionist. It was Ripert, Bourdain's friend of 20 years, who found him hanging in his bathroom at the hotel in a small village near Alsace. As soon as the news broke, social media and all the news networks went into overdrive. Fans of Bourdain's various shows over the years lamented the loss of a friend, for that's what he had become when he brought the world's culinary delights – wondrous and bewildering – to our living rooms.

The world believes that people who seem to have everything – fame, fortune, success, worldwide adoration – do not just kill themselves without showing any signs of being troubled. But they do, especially when their minds are in turmoil. Bourdain did. So did Kate Spade and Robin Williams and countless others before them, and since then. Too often, we read about suicides, and how those closest to the decedent never suspected a thing.

The week after, while mourning the loss of my all-time favourite television host, I contemplated my personal relationship with suicide, how it was both a friend I embraced and an enemy I had to reject. In my search for answers about Anthony Bourdain, which, by the second or third day had become an obsession, I found banner after banner about suicide prevention appearing on various pages, all with encouraging messages and hotline phone numbers to call. There were also messages about looking for warning signs in friends and relatives who might be at risk. How odd, I had thought then, because neither Bourdain nor Spade showed warning signs. Nor had I, in the days and hours before my first attempt.

I also found it puzzling that someone would choose to commit suicide just because a media celebrity had recently done so, and was shocked and fascinated by the information at the same time.

Evidently, a highly-publicised death of a media celebrity often results in a spike in copycat, or emulation, suicides, and is known as the Werther effect, from the character in Goethe's novel, *The Sorrows of Young Werther.* The association between the media and suicide arose from this novel, in which Werther shoots himself with a pistol after he is rejected by the woman he loves. Soon after it was published in the 18th century, there were reports of young men in despair and having lost all hope, killing themselves using the same method.

There are several studies from various countries, including Hong Kong, Japan, Korea and the United States of America, which show that media coverage of celebrity suicides results in significantly higher suicide rates within the population, compared with non-celebrity suicides. One such study[1] in Hong Kong examined the impact on suicides following the death of Leslie Cheung, a famous and immensely popular pop singer and actor who jumped to his death from the 24th floor of the Mandarin Oriental Hotel on 1st April 2003. Just before his death, he had written a short note, which was found inside his jacket pocket:

"Depression! Thank you to the fans. Thank you to Prof Mike (his psychiatrist). *It has been a year of suffering. Thank you, Mr Tong* (his companion), *Thank you Fei Che* (Lydia Sum Tin Ha). *In my life I have done nothing wrong. Why it has to be like this?"*

Predictably, media coverage was extensive and heavily dramatised. Using data on suicides obtained from the Hong

---

1 *Journal of Affective Disorders*, August 2006. Paul Siu Fai Yip, University of Hong Kong.

Kong Census and Statistics Department, as well as case files and suicide notes of people who died by suicide in 2003, the study showed that there was a significant increase in suicides following the death of Leslie Cheung, compared with the average over the preceding three months as well as the corresponding monthly average during 1998–2002. The data included a number of males, aged 25–39 years, many of whom died by jumping. Leslie Cheung was mentioned in case files and suicide notes.

According to a study published in early 2018,[2] news of Robin Williams' death was followed by a nearly 10 per cent increase in the number of suicides in the United States. That increase was especially large among men aged 30 to 44, whose suicide rate rose almost 13 per cent. Even more significant was a 32.3 per cent spike in the number of suicides by hanging, which is how Williams died.

Copycat suicides are a phenomenon sometimes known as "suicide contagion." After a highly publicised suicide, a vulnerable person, who may or may not identify with the deceased celebrity, would see suicide as a solution to their problems. Such people do not have to be afflicted with a mental illness to consider or commit suicide. Often, the impetus to go is as simple as thinking:

"With all that fame and wealth, they still could not cope with life. What hope is there for me?"

For all the years I have spent contemplating suicide, going so far as trying to kill myself, and for all the times I have been curious about the motivation for someone else's suicide, it never

---

2   Plos One. www.journals.plos.org, February 2018. Fink DS, Santaella-Tenorio J.

once occurred to me to follow in the footsteps of a celebrity who had recently committed suicide. I was baffled by the constant messages which popped up every time I did an internet search which included the word "suicide". In Singapore, more than two years after the deaths of Kate Spade and Anthony Bourdain, Google still shows, at the top of the page, a banner with a headline that says, *"Help is available"* and *"Speak with a counsellor today"*, followed by a toll-free phone number in large, bold text.

Then again, it is not surprising, given that every day, at least one person in Singapore takes his own life.

Chapter 8

All too often, after a famous suicide is reported in the media, people offer their opinions, which can be disparaging, no matter how they couch their words. How selfish, how thoughtless, what a coward. Not all comments denigrate the decedent; many are also sympathetic. Either way, they both come from an increasing number of vocal commenters on social media.

I can understand why people think suicide is selfish; suicide leaves friends and families bereft, sometimes blaming themselves, wondering what they could have done to prevent such a violent and untimely death. A suicide is not always thoughtless, considering how some people plan and execute their suicide. They would very likely have thought about the ones left behind. There is nothing cowardly about taking oneself to the unknown, especially for those holding on to their religious faith, knowing that suicide is an unforgivable sin.

Yet, worldwide, 800,000 people commit suicide every year, or one person every 40 seconds.[1] According to the World Health Organisation, there is reason to believe that for each adult who died by suicide there may have been more than 20

---

1   World Health Organisation Sept 2019 https://www.who.int/news-room/fact-sheets/detail/suicide

others attempting suicide. There are no figures to indicate how many seriously consider suicide, but do not get to the point of attempting suicide, or hold back at the last minute. I have been one of the 20 others attempting suicide, just once. I have also been the non-statistic for considering suicide, but not attempting it.

Less than a year after my first diagnosis, and after my first suicide attempt, I was struck by another irresistible urge to die. We were in the middle of house-hunting due to our condominium's imminent en-bloc sale and I was still having trouble coping with my new, more subdued self. My husband dragged me to the doctor's office that Saturday and within a few minutes of talking, my doctor decided that I needed electroconvulsive therapy, better known as ECT, something I had only ever known as shock treatment. In the rare instances I had watched an ECT scene in movies or on television, it had looked barbaric and cruel, with the patient remaining in hospital, lifeless and melancholic. I refused. I'd much rather die, I said. Without ECT, you just might, the doctor shot back, and went on to explain that the treatment was nothing like what is portrayed in film. He assured me that modern methods have made ECT very safe and effective, and explained the procedure. He would inject an anaesthetic and a muscle relaxant before administering a miniscule amount of electricity through my brain to trigger a seizure. It would all take less than five minutes, after which I would be wheeled to my room for some rest, and be ready to be discharged when I woke up, typically about two hours later. The doctor prescribed three sessions starting on Monday, followed by one session each on Wednesday and Friday.

Knowing I had to stay alive, it did not take long before I was convinced that ECT was my only option. Doing the treatment as an outpatient required my husband to sign a document stating that I would be in his care for the whole week, which, in turn, required him to ask that he be taken off all his scheduled flights for that week.

By the time I woke up after the third and last treatment, I thought I would never be the same again. I felt as if I had been to hell and back several times, and would never be allowed to forget the experience. My head hurt, and, moving at a sluggish pace, I felt like I was living out scenes in a slow-motion movie. At times, I could not tell what was real, and what was imagined. Those feelings dissipated within hours – I did not experience any other side effects that week. Not long after, however, the side effect I feared most, hit me without warning. During a family conversation about a holiday six weeks earlier, I realised I could not remember anything about it. My husband showed me some photographs, but nothing returned. He asked me about Christmas, just two months before. I remembered many details, which was reassuring, but being unable to remember the family holiday, I felt robbed of my memory, as if someone had crept into my head and removed a disk from a specific period in my recent history. The doctor said my memory would very likely return after a few months. That memory never did.

By the end of the first year of taking mood-stabilising drugs daily, I learnt that mood stabilisers are not magic bullets; I still had lapses and experienced mainly manic episodes. When I asked my doctor why this was still happening, despite the drugs and adjustments in my lifestyle, he explained that mood stabilisers help to significantly reduce the symptoms of mania and depression, but sometimes, certain triggers could lead to a relapse. Most of the time, I could not remember the triggers, only my reaction, which was usually outrage, followed by extreme shame and uncontrollable sobbing. The doctor would then prescribe a different medication, usually an anti-psychotic, to take along with the mood stabiliser.

In the first seven years of my diagnosis, I saw three doctors, all in private practice. I never felt that they were particularly interested in me as a person who was unwell and determined to get better. The visits lasted between five and 15 minutes, sometimes longer if I had experienced an episode between visits. By the time I had seen the third doctor, I was resigned to the fact that they were only there to monitor my response to medication and to continue the prescription, or add a new one, accordingly.

Then, while I was waiting at the television studio to be interviewed by Channel News Asia for the launch of my memoir, *Praying to the Goddess of Mercy,* I met a doctor, who said that he was representing the Institute of Mental Health (IMH) on the same show. We introduced ourselves and I was immediately struck by his gentleness and warmth. After the interview, having observed how he answered the questions, I decided that I needed to see him. I called IMH as soon as I came home and made an appointment to see this doctor I had just met, after which I cancelled an upcoming appointment with the doctor I had seen for a few years until then. Three weeks later, I was officially a patient at IMH. My medication remained the same – lithium, supplemented by quetiapine when needed – but my dosage varied based on evaluations during my visit. I felt more stable for longer periods after seeing this doctor.

Three years later, this doctor returned to England with his family. I was very upset when he told me, but he assured me that I would be seeing a doctor with whom he was sure I would be very comfortable. I trusted his judgement, and indeed, the doctor who replaced him was equally good. I knew I was in good hands.

Despite receiving the best care, and being conscientious about my medication, I still had lapses. Every now and then, I had days when all I wanted was to die. Sometimes, it was a yearning, which usually transformed into an urge. I could never understand why, and did not care to find out. At that time, whether for a few minutes or a few days, I just knew without any doubt that death was what I wanted and needed.

Chapter 9

In the aftermath of a suicide, bereaved families and friends are usually left struggling to make sense of what went wrong. In the process of trying to understand the unexpected and tragic loss of life, some people are eager to assign blame, sometimes pointing the finger at themselves, while sometimes, channelling the blame towards others. When a well-known and much loved celebrity commits suicide, the whole world is desperate for a reason, and blame probably makes their grief easier to process. Immediately after Anthony Bourdain's suicide, fans pointed the finger at his girlfriend, Asia Argento, calling her a murderer and claiming that widely published photographs of her holding hands with another man had thrown Bourdain into a severe depressive state. This allegation, though unproven, is still mentioned in reference to Bourdain's suicide.

When the gifted poet and novelist Sylvia Plath killed herself at the age of 30, feminists and admirers were quick to vilify her husband, Ted Hughes, who had earlier left Plath for another woman. Their wrath led to Plath's tombstone being defaced, to remove "Hughes" from her name. Each time, Ted Hughes either repaired or replaced the tombstone, at times, in between, removing it for extended periods, to avoid the repeated vandalism. For nearly 35 years until his death in 1998, Hughes lived with being blamed for his wife's death, including being heckled at talks and labelled a murderer.

It is quite likely that since her death, every single paper written about Sylvia Plath has mentioned her suicide, while celebrating her genius. More so, when some of her best works were published posthumously: most notably *Ariel*, published in 1965, and which catapulted Plath to fame; *Crossing the Water*, published in 1971; and *The Collected Poems*, published in 1981, and which won a Pulitzer Prize for poetry. The only novel she wrote was a fictionalised account of her life – *The Bell Jar*, published in January 1963, a month before Plath's death. The novel, now famous and studied in high schools worldwide, was published at that time under a pseudonym and received, at best, a lukewarm response.

Before she died, Plath had been a prolific poet, but it was Hughes who was a much-published, critically-acclaimed and well-known writer, even working on programmes for the BBC, producing essays and talks. They met in early 1956 while Plath, an American, was studying in Cambridge on a Fulbright scholarship. By June that year, they were married. Plath had not told Hughes about her diagnosis and treatment of depression at the age of 20. Nor did she tell him about her various suicide attempts.

In the summer of 1953, after Plath returned from an internship in New York City, her mother learnt that Plath had slashed her legs. Apparently, Plath had wanted to see if "she had the guts to kill herself". Her mother took her to a family physician, who then referred her to a psychiatrist. Plath received her first of several outpatient electroconvulsive treatments in the psychiatrist's office, without anaesthesia or muscle relaxants which was not uncommon in the '50s. In a letter to her pen-pal soon after she had completed the sessions, Plath wrote: *"... a rather brief and traumatic experience of badly-given shock treatment"*, and, *"pretty soon, the only doubt in my mind was the precise time and method of committing suicide."*[1]

Barely a month after her first electroconvulsive treatment, Plath made her first suicide attempt. Distraught over not being accepted for a summer writing programme at Harvard University, Plath went to the basement of her mother's house and tried to kill herself by taking several sleeping pills. She was found alive two days later and admitted to McLean Hospital, one of the top psychiatric hospitals in America. Plath was a few months short of her 20th birthday when she was officially diagnosed as having depression, associated with overwork and failing to be accepted into the Harvard programme. She spent four months at the hospital and made a good recovery after receiving another course of electroconvulsive therapy and psychotherapy.

Sylvia Plath had always been an over-achiever and was a star student in high school, winning a full scholarship to Smith College where she graduated with the highest honours, before winning a Fulbright scholarship to Cambridge. She was successful, attractive and had a bright future. But it all changed when she met and married Ted Hughes in 1956. By all accounts,

---

1 Sylvia Plath, unsent letter to Eddie Cohen, 1953. Published in *Letters Home*, HarpPeren (1992).

they had a good, maybe even vibrant, marriage. A year after they were married, the couple moved to America, where Plath taught at her alma mater. Finding it challenging to write while teaching full-time, Plath and Hughes moved to Boston a year later, where Plath took a job as a receptionist and attended creative seminars in the evenings conducted by the poet Robert Lowell and attended by fellow poet Anne Sexton, whom Plath admired. Both Lowell and Sexton encouraged Plath to write from her personal experience, which she did.

At the end of 1959, Plath and Hughes moved back to England. Their first child, a daughter, was born a month later, followed by the birth of their son two years later. When their son was just six months old, Plath drove her car off the road and into a river, an event she described as a suicide attempt. At around the same time, Plath discovered her husband's affair, and they separated, although he continued to visit her. Within weeks, Plath experienced explosive bursts of creativity and plunged into writing, culminating in what is now most of the poems in *Ariel*.

In early 1963, England experienced one of the coldest winters in a hundred years. Plath's children – two-year-old daughter and baby son – were often sick. In January, nearly 10 years after she was first diagnosed with depression, Plath consulted her GP, Dr Horder, and told him she was feeling depressed, mentioning for the first time the suicide attempt with sleeping pills at her mother's house.[2] She spoke of her marital situation, and described alternating between feeling hopeful and despondent. Plath told Dr Horder that during this time – at least six months – she had

2   "Sylvia Plath and The Depression Continuum", *Journal of the Royal Society of Medicine.* PMC539515

continued writing and recording poetry for the BBC. But now, she felt severely depressed, was often agitated, and often thought about suicide. She was finding it hard just coping with daily life. Dr Horder prescribed an antidepressant and made arrangements to keep in touch with her daily. He also arranged a psychiatric outpatient appointment.

A few close friends, who had rallied round Plath to help with the care of her two small children, later described Plath as being "hysterical" over the breakdown of her marriage, blaming it entirely on Hughes' infidelity and the coldness towards her from his family and friends. Even though she was distressed, Plath took the trouble to maintain her grooming regime and presented herself elegantly. In mid-February, shortly before her outpatient psychiatric appointment was due, Plath was found dead in her own kitchen, with her head in the oven and the gas turned on. An inquiry the next day ruled Plath's death as suicide: meticulously planned, while ensuring the safety of her two young children in the next room.

Sylvia Plath's suicide immortalised her legacy as a tormented poet who, though brilliant, was not quite as successful a writer in her lifetime. Despite being blamed for Plath's suicide, her widower husband, the late Ted Hughes, on the other hand, had gone on to achieve even more success and fame, being appointed Poet Laureate in 1984 and ranked one of the greatest writers of the 20th century. It is easy, satisfying even, to demonise a person for someone's suicide, especially when someone's actions caused despair so intense that it led to suicide. Speculation, judgement and blame typically occur immediately after a suicide, with blame lasting for decades, as is still the case with Ted Hughes, more than 20 years after his death and nearly 60 years after Plath's suicide. But Hughes did not kill Sylvia Plath. Depression did.

I have been, and am, battling depression ... I am now flooded with despair, almost hysteria, as if I were smothering. As if a great muscular owl were sitting on my chest, its talons clenching & constricting my heart.[3]

In the depths of my own despair, and sometimes during an anxiety attack, I, too, have felt this clenching and constricting in my heart, like a knife with a curved tip slicing through and pulling away. I have also felt, at other times, a loudness and turbulence in my head, which I know dissipates eventually, usually within minutes. At such times, suicide appeals to my need to avoid ever experiencing such pain, no matter how fleeting.

Nearly a billion people globally, and from all walks of life, are afflicted with a mental disorder. With suicide claiming on average 800,000 lives annually, it is one of the leading causes of death amongst young people between the ages of 15 and 29 years.[4]

If ever I were to kill myself, if ever my suicide, like Plath's and millions before and since her death, were triggered by an intense desperation resulting from something someone did or might have done, no one would, nor should, ever be blamed.

If ever I were to kill myself, my suicide should only be blamed on my mental illness.

---

3   *The Journals of Sylvia Plath*, Anchor. Abridged edition (1998).
4   World Health Organisation News Release 07-10-20 Global challenge for movement on mental health.

Chapter 10

Being on medication for bipolar disorder simply means that I am being treated for a mental illness. It does not mean that I am cured, or will ever be cured. There is currently no cure for mental illness, and until a cure is found, if ever, I must continue to take my medication daily.

No matter how diligent I am about taking my mood stabilisers, there have been, and will continue to be, lapses in my moods. On most days, I feel normal, or as close to what "normal" is supposed to mean – I am neither restless, short-tempered or energetic, nor am I listless and sad. But there are still days when I wake up feeling fine, ready for another predictable, uneventful day, and someone says something, or does something, and it triggers a reaction, one that comes quickly and unexpectedly. This usually happens when something does not go according to plan and I do not feel equipped to handle the situation. And it is almost always something seemingly insignificant.

It could be something like finding out just before lunch that I cannot prepare something specific for my family because the ingredients have either rotted or I forgot to buy them. For most people, this would not be a problem – Singapore is full of options, from takeaway at the countless hawker stalls within a two-kilometre radius, to delivery from hundreds of restaurants island-wide. For me, it throws my mind into a spin, because I now have to change my plans. Where once, a long time ago, I thrived on spontaneity and impulse, I now need predictability. Something inconsequential to most people – what to have for lunch – becomes an event for me, so when something goes wrong, I feel helpless and a failure. In a situation like this, my mind feels like it is working hard to come up with a solution, while wanting to shut down at the same time. I take deep breaths, and sometimes it works, and I start to rummage in the fridge or freezer to whip up a simple meal quickly. Sometimes, I begin to weep, only to burst into a sob within seconds, feeling incapable of taking care of myself, and my family. When I say to myself that I want to, or need to, run away, I know that what I really mean is that I want to die.

Once lunch is over, and I feel better, I replay the entire episode in my head. Do I really want to die? Surely not; it was a small thing, in fact, nothing, really. Just lunch that went wrong and then it was fixed. No one dies because lunch did not go according to plan. But this is not about lunch. It is rarely ever about the situation itself. It is all about how I respond to the situation, specifically, the effect it has on me. Almost always, it is beyond my control, no matter how hard I try. And yes, when it is all happening, I do feel like I want to die. But by the time it's over, I no longer feel suicidal.

In the last 15 years since my diagnosis, I have done whatever I thought I needed to do to maintain stability in my mind.

Being diligent about medication was my first step. While I had a tight and reliable circle of family and friends, I have also learnt to rely on myself to eliminate sources of stress and anxiety. This is not always easy, especially as there are situations I cannot foresee, or worse, situations that I cannot control.

From around 2009 until 2013, I experienced more frequent and longer periods of stability than in the years before that. I counted my episodes in terms of months and years. Typically, I would see my doctor every two months, and often, have nothing significant to report. He would prescribe the usual dosage of lithium, which was 800mg at that time, and arrange to see me in another two months. In that next appointment, I would report an incident or two, which made me manic or depressive. At those appointments, I told my doctor that I self-medicated with the anti-psychotics he prescribed for me to take as needed, which was maybe once or twice every two months.

Then, in 2014, and for the next six years, I spent more time mulling over suicide than I had in all the years before.

In 2013, five years since I had switched from various drugs to lithium, I felt more stable than I could remember. A year earlier, I had returned to Singapore after spending two years in Bali, where I had owned and managed a Bed and Breakfast. My first book, *Praying to the Goddess of Mercy, A Memoir of Mood Swings*, was published soon after my return. It received good reviews and much publicity, resulting in excellent sales. I was happy and I felt what it was like to be well and truly alive. I had not experienced an episode in months. I was by then a patient at the Institute of Mental Health and had finally found a doctor that, for the first time, I trusted completely.

With my first book being a success, I decided to try writing fiction. Negative sentiments against migrant workers prompted me to write a story about migrants, from whom most Singaporeans are descended. As I was always fascinated by the early days leading to Singapore's independence, I decided to set my novel beginning in the early '60s. The book required hours of research, both online and at the library. I also visited the National Museum several times to learn more about the colonial government before Singapore gained full internal self-government in 1959. I had not expected to be quite so enlightened in the process of research, but I was, which made writing the novel so much more enjoyable, and I dedicated every afternoon to writing. By now, I had been relatively stable for over a year. Things were looking good.

Then, sometime in August, I had lunch with a close friend. Her husband was a pilot with Singapore Airlines, just like my husband. The difference was that her husband was a Singapore citizen and mine was a permanent resident. My friend's husband had told her that he had heard a rumour that Singapore Airlines would not be offering re-employment to pilots who were permanent residents when they retired at the age of 62. This meant my husband had less than two years with a company he had worked with since he arrived as a 23-year-old in 1977. I felt anxious, wanting to go home immediately to tell him what I had just heard.

My husband was not sure what to make of this news. It was probably just a rumour, he said, but considering Singapore Airlines had blamed the global financial crisis of 2007/2009 for retrenching more than 70 expatriate pilots in January that year, he was concerned. One of those expatriate pilots was a close family friend who had moved to Abu Dhabi two months earlier to fly for Etihad. My husband was not ready to retire at 62, and, based on his company's revised policy, which was in line with the government's direction, expected to continue until the maximum age of 65. If there was even the slightest truth to the rumour, my husband wanted to be prepared. He arranged to meet his Chief Pilot, who assured my husband that the company was doing fine, that there were no plans to retire pilots at 62 and, more importantly, if the situation were to change, the decision on re-employment would not be based on citizenship. This meant that if re-employment was not going to be offered, both citizens and permanent residents would be equally affected.

I was sceptical, and we discussed the possibility of losing his job. The anxiety of my husband possibly retiring in less than two years caused me sleepless nights. I was not as worried about financial security, and was more concerned about my husband not being ready to stop flying at the age of 62. He was one of very few pilots I knew who genuinely loved to fly.

A week or two later, with my anxiety levels fluctuating wildly, I stopped writing. Even after the assurance from my husband's boss that things were looking much better for Singapore Airlines, I was simply not convinced that his job was safe. The company was, after all, a business. If something happened to cause profits to dip again, another round of retrenchments was possible. We considered his options. Very few airlines hired non-citizens as captains. Fewer still hired anyone above the age of 60. His best chances were the Gulf carriers, namely Emirates, Qatar and Etihad. If he were to lose his job with Singapore Airlines and had to move to the Gulf, I wanted to go with him.

Back then, we were living in Siglap. It was a beautiful three-storey house, cocooned within lush palms and cinnamon trees. One of the conditions of my husband's application to buy the house jointly with me was that, as a permanent resident, he could not rent it out. Even if, for some reason, I decided against moving with him to wherever he found a job, I would not have wanted to live alone in that house. As renting it out was not an option, I suggested we put it up for sale, and buy a condominium where there were no restrictions on ownership.

It was something we had to think about very carefully, as we loved our home, and were contented living in Siglap. After much deliberation over the next few days, we decided it was best that we sell our house and move to a condominium. This meant that if my husband were to lose his job and move overseas, we could rent out our home. And if he could keep his job until the age of 65, all the better.

The house was sold within a few weeks of being put on the market. We then began the tedious task of looking for a new home in a condominium. The endless viewings wore me down. Nothing could replace the privacy, tranquillity and resort-like ambience of our current home. After spending several hours in the afternoons on viewings, I found it hard to be calm in the evenings. I started taking anti-psychotics every few days, to help me sleep and be calm the next day. We had 12 weeks from the confirmation of the sale before we had to move out. Those 12 weeks included finding a place, and renovating it, which was usually necessary. We favoured the East Coast area but my husband's criteria, few but very specific – a spacious balcony, privacy, quietness – made it a huge challenge to find anything suitable. Eventually, we found a flat that met our needs and we moved to our new home in early 2014.

It was the beginning of one of my most difficult years since I began taking medication for bipolar disorder.

Chapter 11

We had just completed the renovations and settled into our new home in early 2014. Within a week, I began to miss my old home, and more than that, my near-daily lunch of hawker food. I am a huge fan of our street-food and in the couple of years before we left Siglap, I had lunch at the various hawker centres and kopitiams in the area as often as five times a week. To avoid the crowds, I would leave my home at around 11 o'clock and, depending on where I was going, I would either walk, take the bus, or ride my bicycle. From where I now lived, it was a 15-minute walk in the heat to the bus stop, a minimum half-hour walk to the nearest hawker centre, and an unnerving bike-ride on narrow, two-way roads. I felt isolated and a bit lost. I realised I could no longer adapt to change quite as easily as I used to, and it irked me.

On the days when my husband was flying, I drove to the Katong-Siglap area for lunch at least three times week. I visited all my favourite haunts, including the stall by Siglap canal for Teochew fishball noodles, the tiny Peranakan stall in Jalan Tua Kong for nasi ulam and chendol, to the kopitiam near the junction of East Coast Road and Telok Kurau for Hokkien mee. It took on average an hour to drive there and back, and, on average, all of 10 minutes to order my meal and finish it. I did this for weeks before I realised how absurd it was, to spend six times more in driving for a meal than at consuming it. But as the whole ritual gave me much comfort, something I needed, I decided I should just take what I could find, and do whatever made me happy. Distance and time were insignificant.

One day, after a trip to Ghim Moh Market, I decided to try the fishball noodles and was immediately hooked. From that day onwards, several months after moving, I sampled various foods at hawker centres and kopitiams closer to my home, from Ghim Moh to ABC Brickworks and everything in between. I stopped driving to Katong and Siglap just to eat. At last, after a few months, I felt settled into my new environment. I was happy.

Then, just as everything was falling into place for me, a family with two young children moved in to the flat above. We soon realised that noise insulation was non-existent. Early in the morning, we heard a child running around in the bedroom above ours, along with things being thrown on the floor. We also heard furniture being dragged at all hours, including late at night. We had not heard such sounds from the previous tenants, except for the infrequent jumping of the three young boys who had lived there. I was very distressed by these sounds and wondered if it was just our unit that was badly constructed, or if other condominiums had a similar problem. I had lived in an HDB flat in Marine Parade for 12 years, and my husband and I had lived in several condominiums for years, and never experienced such noise from our neighbours.

Unable to bear the racket, especially when it started before seven in the morning, and thinking perhaps we were being overly sensitive, I asked my neighbours downstairs if they heard our footsteps and other noise from our flat. She said no, she thought we were hardly at home. I laughed, and assured her we must just be quiet people. One particularly noisy afternoon, still allowing for the possibility that I had over-sensitive hearing, I emailed 16 friends to ask about noise from their neighbours upstairs. All of them had lived, or were still living, in condominiums in Singapore, including new luxury condominiums, HDB and old walk-up flats. Every single friend responded, and most said they sometimes heard footsteps and other sounds but it wasn't usually a problem. "Usually", when I asked, meant that either the neighbours were naturally light-footed; or when told about the sounds from their flat, the neighbours were apologetic and made an effort to reduce them; or that my friends, whether tenants or landlords, were lucky to have quiet people living upstairs, like the previous tenants.

The feedback from one of those friends surprised me – she had lived at Ardmore Park, a luxury condominium near Orchard Road, and soon after a family had moved in above her home, she had begun to hear a squeaky sound every afternoon, around four o'clock, when the kids usually came home from school. It was a grating sound, and having tolerated it for weeks, my friend went upstairs to speak to her neighbour. Turns out, it was the sound of a kid on his tricycle. I was shocked that such a sound could go through the concrete, probably due to poor construction without sound insulation. I could not understand how such places could fetch high rentals with inferior construction, and rely on residents to be quiet.

Their responses gave me the reassurance I needed; I no longer thought the problem was caused by sensitive hearing, although being able to tune out sounds is a gift some people have and I must have missed it when it was being handed out. Most of them suggested I speak to my neighbour, which I did. I also sent him a number of felt pads for his furniture, and bought myself every type of ear plugs I could find in the shops, none of which were effective. I researched the best ones and found that they were only available in America; a close friend then sent me a box of 16 pieces via a two-day courier service. There was little improvement, after which my husband suggested we write to our neighbour, to avoid confrontation. Things improved, but it did not last. I resorted to calling the management office, and asked the manager to come over and listen. I asked her if the sounds were as loud for her as they were for me. Yes, it was, she had said, and agreed to speak to the neighbours. Once again, the noise reduced but not for long.

For several hours in the late morning and early afternoon, while the children from upstairs were in school, I resumed writing my novel. It had been nearly a year since I had written, so I needed to re-read it before resuming writing my novel. I had not realised that I had written more than 60,000 words at that point, enough for a full novel. But there was so much more that I had wanted to write about, which gave me impetus to start then and there.

Several months later, I was invited to a Diwali dinner organised by a few women in the condominium. It was held by the pool, and most of the people were residents at the condominium. I asked about noise from their neighbours upstairs. The response was much like the ones from friends, except a few men and women told me that they did not realise how noisy they or their children had been until a security guard arrived at their flat. They had said they wished the neighbour had told them directly, instead of calling the security guard. At that time, it had never occurred to me to call the security guards. When the issue first surfaced, I had spoken directly to the resident, then to the condominium manager, then I had written to him, and finally, when nothing seemed to work and realising that there was nothing I could do, I decided that I would learn to live with the noise. I knew it was not going to be easy, but I also knew that I owed it to myself and my family to try my hardest. My mental health was at stake.

* * *

About a week before Christmas, my husband received his contract for re-employment. It meant that he would not have to retire upon turning 62, which was in just over three months, and that he would be re-employed on a lower salary, and on a one-year contract, renewable annually until he turned 65. He signed the contract and hand-delivered it the next day. I had a bad feeling about the contract, and read it while he was out. When he came home, I told him that I would not be surprised if Singapore Airlines withdrew this offer or terminated his contract with one month's notice soon after he started working under the new terms, when it would be way too late to go anywhere else. My husband, ever the optimist, said they would not do that. By offering him the contract at this point, they must have planned in advance and expected to need pilots for the next year.

Three weeks later, just after he returned home from the simulator – my husband was a training captain – he received a call from another captain, who asked if he had seen an email about a meeting the next day, and if my husband knew what it might be about. The next day, my husband left for the meeting after lunch, saying he would be home in time for us to go to the cinema as planned. He came home nearly two hours later, saying we would not be going out that night. He looked troubled as soon as he walked in; I knew right then, before he told me: Singapore Airlines would not be offering re-employment to pilots past the age of 62. He was going to be out of a job in 10 weeks. Even though I had half-expected something like this to happen, I had not expected it to be quite so soon. My husband's stoicism – legendary amongst family and close friends – helped to keep me calm on the outside, but deep down, I felt desperate to hold on to a world that was starting to slowly crumble around me.

Chapter 12

In early April 2015, our daughter and I drove my husband to the airport, from where he was scheduled to fly to Addis Ababa via Bangkok. It was going to be another 10 weeks of training before he would be back on home leave. I could not bear the thought of him being so far away, for so long, but I managed to put on a brave face. From the moment my husband had left for his interview with Ethiopian Airlines, I researched everything I needed to know about a country best remembered amongst my generation for a biblical famine that brought together the world's greatest musicians for Live Aid, a benefit concert broadcast globally and viewed by over a billion people. What was then a military dictatorship backed by the Soviet Union, and in the midst of a civil war which terrorised and killed civilians, Ethiopia had since become a democracy and founder of the African Union, comprising 55 member states in Africa. I also researched Ethiopian Airlines and having learnt that it was an established airline with a young, modern fleet and a decent safety record, felt it was good enough for my husband. Even then, with all the factors having been considered, and having accepted that Ethiopia and its national airline were both safe, I worried about him going to work in a most unfamiliar place, with unfamiliar systems and customs.

The day he left was difficult for all of us, knowing that he would not be home for more than two months. We had video calls several times a week. The hotel and food were acceptable at best, which I knew meant that they were not very good; my husband was tolerant about many things, but I felt badly for him, having to merely bear with the food and accommodation for two months.

As it turned out, it was almost three months before my husband came home. He had missed home-cooked food and for the 10 days that he was home, I wanted to go all out to make him his favourite food. I planned a menu and shopped for fresh ingredients every other day. I played the happy home-maker for breakfast, lunch and dinner. I enjoyed taking care of my husband, making him the centre of my universe. I did not make any plans to see my friends while he was home. We went to the movies, we had a few restaurant meals, like chicken rice and nasi lemak. He did not ask, nor expect any of this, but I felt it was a small indulgence which he deserved. I was happier than I had been since before he had left for Ethiopia. Then, all too soon, his 10 days were up and he had to return to work. As soon as I woke up the next morning, I felt my husband's absence, but the void I felt only hit me as I was about to prepare my lunch. I wondered how I would manage for the next three years. I had to, and resolved to cope with my family's new situation, just as my husband was coping with his new life so he could continue flying.

In those early months, joy at my husband's monthly visit home did not cross over into mania, nor did sorrow at his departure become depression. To ensure I remained stable and coped with my new situation, my doctor maintained my dosage of quetiapine, the anti-psychotic, on an as-needed basis. This meant taking it more frequently, and instead of once or twice a month, I took it once, sometimes twice, a week. When I found I needed more, I halved the dosage to 12.5mg and took it every few days, which helped me maintain my stability, without making me feel listless, for the next few cycles of my husband's departure to and return from Ethiopia.

Not long after my husband left for Ethiopia, I began to feel his absence with greater intensity. Having spent more than half my life with him, while he travelled for a living, I had grown accustomed to him being away for days on end, but not for three weeks at a stretch. I set aside five hours every afternoon to writing, re-writing and editing my novel. Restlessness for a few evenings in a row led to binge-watching television shows, followed by going to sleep at around 11 o'clock and waking up at around seven o'clock. The first two doctors I had seen after my diagnosis emphasised the importance of sleep, and over the years, I found that to maintain stability in my mind, I needed around 10 hours of sleep.

Unfortunately, with the noise upstairs starting before seven o'clock, I was deprived of my 10 hours of sleep. None of the ear plugs I had tried were effective. Sometimes, I went back to sleep after things quietened down an hour later, but most times, I could not. I tried sleeping earlier, but my evenings felt too short. I tried afternoon naps but it got in the way of my writing, and I was keen to finish my novel.

One afternoon, the noise, which had by now become more frequent and lasted for longer stretches, affected me more than it had since the family moved in a year before. The sounds and the volume that came crashing through the ceiling – kids running and jumping, throwing things on the floor – were no different from all the other days. But I was different that day. Feeling restless, eager to get some work done but unable to think and write from the distraction, I called the hospital to arrange an emergency appointment with my doctor. The earliest he could see me was weeks away. As I could not contact him directly, and I did not want to see another doctor through the emergency department, I sent a message through the hospital's website, asking for the message to be forwarded to the doctor. I do not remember the exact words, but I distinctly remember saying that I could no longer tolerate the noise from my neighbours, and that I wish I had a gun, and that I wanted to shoot myself. I ended the message by asking for help. I did not re-read the message before sending it but I will always remember the gist of that message, probably because I was by then in great distress, just longing for the peace and quiet the rest of the residents in my neighbourhood enjoyed.

Right after I sent the message, I laid on the couch and sobbed, looking at the ceiling and cursing the residents in the floor above. I caught myself, and felt badly about sending bad vibes towards children who were simply expending their energy and not being taught by their parents the concept of consideration. My sobs abated, I sat up, and faced my laptop. I saved my work, closed my computer, went to the kitchen to pour myself a Diet Coke and sat on the kitchen floor, still crying, and thought about how I would kill myself that night. Just then, the phone rang. It was my doctor, asking if I could go to the hospital immediately. It was nearly four o'clock, the end of consultation hours, but he would set aside time for me. Unable to drive, I called for a taxi. On the ride to the hospital, I focused on a new character I was about to create in my novel.

As in previous visits, when the issue of my noisy neighbours was always mentioned, my doctor suggested mediation. Not an option, I said. I was terrified of him and could not bear to face him. I would rather die, I said. My distress plain to see, my doctor then suggested I take quetiapine more frequently, an anti-psychotic I had taken for years as-needed, just so I could catch up on sleep every few days. It worked. I took it two or three times a week and slept soundly for about 12 hours. I no longer felt suicidal. But it was not sustainable. I was usually listless for several hours after waking. Writing on those days was difficult, and I could only manage writing for two hours at the most, often distracted, with the rest of the time staring out into space, my mind blank.

Eager to finish my novel, I stopped taking the quetiapine and stayed on my prescribed lithium dosage. The noise continued, sometimes worse, sometimes a little better. The early morning din remained constant. When it got particularly bad, the sleeplessness returned, and along with it, the irritability, which, within days, turned into anguish. After several letters from us, with copies to the management office, I realised neither I nor the management office could do anything more. I researched solutions on social media and found that apart from mediation and approaching the neighbour, the options were hostile, including using subwoofers to drown their flat with bass frequencies and vibrations while we went out, and ceiling thumpers. I was tempted to try the subwoofers, but my husband and children live by a code of exceptional decency and quashed the idea without further discussion. As I had done since the neighbours moved in, I learnt to somehow bear the noise.

A few weeks later, while I was struggling to write, hoping to finish just one chapter that afternoon, I heard the heavy thumping of children jumping. They might have had a friend or two over to play, because it sounded like quite a few feet jumping and landing at various times, the sound pounding through my ceiling, only to repeat these movements again and again. I used to wonder how much sugar must be in their diet, to have that much energy to expend. I also used to wonder why, knowing how noisy the children were, the parents did not ask them to jump just outside their flat, where the lift lobby was spacious and safe. I no longer wondered, because I believed they simply did not care. I despaired, not knowing what to do. Neither my husband nor I had ever asked for special treatment; only the peace and quiet that other residents expected and received. I thought about calling the police, but from some of the news reports I had read about neighbours from hell, the police would probably not be able to do anything. Worse, I feared that the neighbours might retaliate and make things worse. I went to my one daughter's bedroom, and then the other daughter's bedroom, but I could still hear the kids jumping.

As I laid on her bed and began to cry, I felt an energy building inside me, starting from my belly and moving slowly to the tips of my fingers and toes. I was not familiar with this sensation, and thought it might be a good thing, like a mysterious power to help me cope with the torment. I stopped crying, and lay still for just a few more minutes, trying to comprehend this effervescence slowly streaming through my body. Battling this unfamiliar sensation, I sat up and took a deep breath before going to the laundry room outside, at the back of the flat. I took the key to the laundry room, unlocked the door, and without a thought, wheeled out the spare cooking gas tank and pushed it towards the domestic helper's room, but stopped when I had trouble lifting it above the step and into the utility area. I left the gas tank aside and went to retrieve a large plastic sheet and some duct tape from a storage container near the laundry room. I looked at the louvred window of the helper's room and figured I could seal it in five minutes. Just as I was about to return to the task of manoeuvring the tank to get it over the step and into the utility area, I heard the buzzer. It was a delivery man with a package for my daughter. I buzzed him up the lift, and waited for him. In the few seconds it had taken him to arrive, I could feel that energy slowly dissipate. After handing the package to me, the delivery man glanced at the tank and asked if I needed help. No, I said, shaking my head, thank you for asking. As he entered the lift, I wheeled the gas tank back to the laundry area, went back into the flat, locked the door behind me, threw the unused plastic sheet down the chute and went to my room. Every action was mechanical and unemotional.

As I laid on my bed, staring at the fan, I tried to evoke that sensation which had crept into me barely 10 minutes earlier. It was a destructive energy, one that had led me to kill myself in a most deliberate manner. It was nothing like the mysterious power that I momentarily believed it was. For months after this incident, I would occasionally think back to that afternoon and wonder if I might have died that day, had it not been for the delivery man. Or would I have changed my mind while I sealed the room, or just before I was overcome by the gas. After a while, it no longer mattered, and I no longer wondered. I simply tried to get on with my life.

After that episode, which I never mentioned to anyone, not even to my doctor, I knew I had to do something about the noise from upstairs. I had gotten much too close to executing an unplanned, impulse-driven suicide and was determined to avoid a similar situation. I needed my sleep, but did not want it to be chemically-induced. After trawling the internet, I decided to hire a professional to record the sounds. The sound engineer arrived at about 5.30am for the set-up to record the peak noise periods – for half an hour before 7am and another hour around 4pm. The report was emailed to me, along with the sound recording, a few days later. I listened to it, using the cues on the report for particularly loud sounds, and then wrote a letter to the management office. I rushed to the management office with the letter, the report and the recording, which I had saved on a thumb drive. The manager played the recording and agreed it was loud. With the evidence, she was forced to agree that it was never about me being intolerant or too sensitive. It was always about them being inconsiderate. My friends from the same condominium had heard these same sounds when visiting. As I left the office, I said to the manager, this has gone on for too long, please make it stop. If the man and his wife did not believe how much noise they were creating, perhaps the recording would motivate them to be a bit more considerate.

It worked. Apparently, they were surprised at how the sounds were amplified from their floor through our ceiling. The man's heavy footsteps continued but the sounds of doors banging, furniture dragging and children jumping, were considerably lower. I was able to get off the anti-psychotics and sleep peacefully. I could write every afternoon. After nearly a year-and-a-half of torment, I was now able to live in my flat peacefully, like everybody else.

Unfortunately, it lasted for only several weeks. It was soon noisy again, but not as bad as it used to be. My husband, when he was back from one of his trips, asked me to somehow live with the noise, and whenever it became unbearable, we would simply write to them, with a copy to the management office, and ask them to be more quiet. Sometimes they obliged, sometimes they did not, but overall, it was no longer quite as bad as it was before. So, I learnt to cope. Every day, while my husband was away and our daughter was at work, I had my routine, something doctors always say is essential – along with medication, sleep, and exercise – for maintaining mental health. I would wake up at around nine o'clock and spend the morning reading, before heading out for my favourite street-food lunch, back home to write my novel, make dinner, watch television or read a book, and went to bed by 10.30pm. Some mornings, I went to the market or supermarket. At least once or twice a week, I met friends for lunch or dinner.

At that point, it was not as if I was suddenly happy, but I was no longer so dispirited, nor angry enough, nor felt helpless, and so I thought much less about suicide. Life was as good as it got for me, and I learnt to navigate it the way I had for decades, which is to say, I lived quite contentedly while focusing on all the good that surrounded me: my family and my friends.

With so much time at my disposal, I continued writing. Picking up from where I had left off, I had expected the words to flow from my mind onto the screen in much the same way as they had when I had first commenced on the manuscript. But it was nothing like that. I had to re-read my manuscript several times to think about what I wanted my characters to say and do, and the situations to which I would lead them. The words and the scenarios were elusive. I then took the bold step of reducing my dosage of lithium, from 800mg a day to 400mg, taking one pill instead of two. On top of that, I sometimes skipped two days of medication, resuming on the third day. After a week, I found it a little easier to write, and within a few weeks, the words came back and I was able to write like I had before.

During a routine visit with my doctor, about a month after I had reduced my dosage, I confessed what I had done. He was appalled. He had always been a supportive doctor, with remarkable empathy, more than any doctor I had ever seen, and being concerned about a possible swing to mania, told me that I had to revert to his prescribed dosage. Then I might as well stop writing, I said. We discussed my writing schedule, and my behavioural pattern in the weeks since I had reduced my dosage. I beseeched him to find a solution that would allow me to write without the risk of a manic or suicidal episode, reminding him that I had been on lithium for more than five years.

After some deliberation, my doctor agreed to alter my regimen. I was to strictly adhere to 800mg a day, every other day.

I had to devise a system to ensure that I did not skip more than a day. I promised absolute compliance and, for the next three or four months of writing and editing, with two visits to my doctor in between, I was able to write with only a few occasions when I felt overwhelmed, or manic, usually triggered by lack of sleep from the noise upstairs. I managed these episodes by increasing the frequency of quetiapine, a very effective anti-psychotic. For two or three days after that, I simply did not write. Instead, I either read, or listened to music, or watched television. Several months following the reduced dosage, I became more erratic, and my doctor insisted I resume my previous dosage. It was more challenging to write while on my full dosage of lithium but I managed, knowing that my mental stability was a priority.

In March 2016, I completed my one-hundred-and-sixteen-thousand-word novel. That very night, I submitted my manuscript to a leading local publisher. In late 2016, my novel, *Rain Tree*, was published by a leading local independent publisher and launched at the Singapore Writers Festival. My husband, our daughter, and several close friends attended the event. I was very happy that day, and for months after that. In between, I had bouts of anxiety and mania, some depression probably, although I do not remember the triggers, nor those moments. I managed to bounce back and not feel suicidal for nearly all of that year. By November, I felt stable enough to start working on another novel.

Chapter 13

The year 2017 started off well. Just before Chinese New Year, my daughter and I flew to America, where we joined my husband and our other daughter, for our annual winter holiday. They had flown in from Ethiopia and England respectively, which made our reunion all the more special. Our friends, with whom we had enjoyed winter holidays for more than two decades, joined us from Minnesota and Texas. As had been the practice for several years, we spent a few days with my mother on our way back home. She had then been living 20 miles south of Los Angeles, for more than 10 years. Those three weeks in America were glorious, and I could not have been happier. I was counting my months of stability and was thankful. With the encouragement I received from my novel, which had sold well, I was ready to resume writing.

In the time between finishing *Rain Tree* and its publication several months later, there had been many articles about William Shakespeare, in honour of his 400th death anniversary. I considered a re-telling of one of his stories, perhaps set in Singapore, and went through a list of his most popular works.

I was keen on one of my favourites, *Hamlet*, but it had been retold in the brilliant novel, *The Story of Edgar Sawtelle*. Besides the predictable works, like *Romeo and Juliet*, there were other possibilities, but I was not sure if I could think of a way to adapt a Shakespearean story and set it in Singapore, with multi-racial characters. It was around this time when I had read a BBC news report a few months earlier about a National Memorial Day in the United Kingdom for victims of honour crimes, defined as any act – emotional abuse, physical assault, kidnap and murder – to defend the honour and reputation of a family. The report focused on the honour killing of a teenager in 2003, whose parents were jailed for their crime.[1]

Years before, I had read snippets of Shakespeare's tragedy, *Titus Andronicus*, a play set towards the end of the Roman Empire, revolving around Titus, a fictional army general, who was hell-bent on revenge against Tamora, Queen of the Goths. Undoubtedly, it is Shakespeare's most violent work, and as a result, one of his least respected plays. While it was very popular in the 16th and 17th centuries, it was condemned and largely ignored, especially in the Victorian era, when it was considered extremely distasteful, and the violence too graphic. The reputation of *Titus Andronicus* began to improve in the middle of the 20th century, when some universities introduced this work in their syllabus and small theatre groups began to stage this tragedy. I bought a copy of the book online and read it in three days, before researching the text to understand some of the verses. It was then that I found a quote by the brilliant writer, T.S. Eliot, which said:

---

1   Shafilea Ahmad was just 17 when she was murdered by her parents, who believed she was too westernised for wanting to wear make-up and go to parties. They were found guilty in 2012 and jailed for life.

*". . . one of the stupidest and most uninspired plays ever
written, a play in which it is incredible that Shakespeare had
any hand at all, a play in which the best passages would be
too highly honoured by the signature of Peele . . ."*

When a Nobel Laureate, whose works influenced some of the
greatest poets and musicians of our time, including Ted Hughes
and Bob Dylan, used the words *"stupidest and most uninspired"*
to describe the work of one of the world's most successful and
timeless writers, I was fascinated. Combined with the Asian love
for gory stories, I knew I had picked the right work. Within days,
I had written a basic plot with characters and scenarios inspired
by *Titus Andronicus*.

By this time, I had been seeing another psychiatrist at IMH,
as the previous doctor had left a few months earlier. I told my
new doctor about my plan to adjust the dosage and frequency as
I had done before. Concerned for my health, he asked me to stay
on the current prescription. He was a conscientious doctor, and
I was a relatively new patient to him, so I understood his need
to be particularly cautious. After that consultation, I decided I
would do as I had done when I wrote the previous book – I would
take the same dosage, and skip a day. If it became a problem,
I would revert to the original prescription, which I did, within
a few months. The next year-and-a-half, beginning in early
2017, was spent on writing and editing during the weeks my
husband was away, and scheduling my breaks while he was
back on home leave. I also saw a few of my friends on days that
I did not feel like writing. For the bigger part of that year, I had
felt happy and stable.

One evening in late 2017, feeling blissful after a wonderful dinner with one of my closest friends, I received a frantic call from an aunt who was visiting my mother in California. She summoned me to resolve care arrangements for my mother, whose dementia was getting worse. At that time, I was already calling my mother twice a day, every day, and was due to call her at 10.30 that night. My aunt handed the phone to my mother, who asked me not to trouble myself, but from her voice, I knew I had to get to her as soon as I possibly could. It was nearly 10 o'clock on a Monday night when I began my frantic search for flights to Los Angeles. After nearly an hour, I managed to find a flight on China Southern via Guangzhou, scheduled to leave in the early hours of Wednesday morning, just 28 hours away.

I booked the flight, spoke to my husband, who was in Liege at that time, and my daughters, and told them I was booked to return in 10 days, but it could be later. All through that long, never-ending flight from Guangzhou to Los Angeles, all I could think of was my inability to care for my 85-year-old mother. I arrived at my mother's house in the early afternoon. My aunt explained that my mother was not eating well, even though there was a woman who came in three times a week to cook Sindhi[2] food for her.

That night, after my mother had gone to sleep, my aunt told me how worried she was about my mother's condition and that, since her arrival a few days earlier, she had been thinking about nothing but my mother's welfare. This aunt was also my mother's closest friend, and to whom my mother had confided her fears and her dreams for decades. She had to leave the next

---

2   Native to the Sindh region of Pakistan. Most Sindhi Hindus fled to India during the 1947 Partition.

day to spend a few days with another relative, hence the urgency to discuss some options for my mother's care. When my aunt suggested in hushed tones that I needed to consider placing my mother in a home, I knew she was right, but I was sure my mother would refuse. As my mother was estranged from both my sisters, I had discussed the possibility of putting her in a home while I was on a visit earlier that year. My mother had insisted that she was capable of looking after herself and would never live in a home. At that time, we had assumed that if my mother had to be placed in a home, it would be somewhere near Los Angeles, where she had built her life in the past 20 years.

My aunt suggested a home in India. She told me about a place at which she had been volunteering for years. It was owned and managed by a Sindhi man, whose mother also lived there. My mother would have the company of 15 other residents, all of whom were Sindhi. I was tired, jet-lagged and desperately needed some sleep. I would think about it, I said, and discuss the matter with my mother after my aunt left to stay with other relatives.

Before speaking to my mother about moving to India, I decided to visit a few homes within a 20-mile radius, to get a sense of what was available and at what cost. I made appointments to view three homes that day and hired a car. The best of the three was at Anaheim, a 20-minute drive from her home and close circle of friends. It was pleasant, perhaps a bit clinical, with caring staff and a diverse resident population. Vegetarian meals were an option but consisted of mainly bland food. This was not going to suit my mother. Besides, she would resent paying US$5,000 a month to be in such a facility.

That evening, I ordered pizza and mentioned the home visits to my mother, who was upset at the idea of leaving her home. I told her about my aunt's recommendation to move to India. She gasped, and said she could not move so far away from her friends and relatives, many of whom she saw regularly. She insisted she was well enough to take care of herself. I tried to convince her she was not. Eventually, after two or three days, she agreed that it was in her best interest to move to India. I was overcome with joy and could not anticipate all the logistics that would accompany such a big move, nor could I see the obstacles that lay ahead. I messaged my husband and daughter to say that I would not be home until a week or two later than planned.

The morning my mother had agreed to go to India, my aunt put me in touch with the manager of the home. He reserved a room starting tentatively in December. I asked my mother's friends about selling her house. I thought it was simply a matter of contacting a realtor and signing some papers. One of her friend's husband told me it was not that simple because, being part of a low-income development – which surprised me because it looked superior to some private apartments I had seen in Singapore – the house had to be sold through the city council, who would determine the price. The next morning, I went to the office with my mother, who had to sign some forms. The price set by the city council was the same as what my mother had paid more than 10 years earlier. Factoring inflation and thousands spent on home improvement, she was about to lose at least 60 per cent of what she had already put into the house. Seeing her sorrow at having to sell her home, and moving halfway across the world, I could not bear to tell her about the financial loss. It did not matter in terms of her security, as her pension and social security were enough for her stay in India. But it affected me; I knew that even with her modest asset, she had hoped to make a profit to leave as an inheritance for me, her two estranged daughters and her two grandchildren. I resolved to make her transition as smooth, and her life as comfortable, as I possibly could.

The house was sold within a few days to an elderly Korean widow who had friends in the same development. By now, I was starting to feel drained from squeezing so much into so little time – inspecting nursing homes, visiting friends and relatives, and making several trips to the town council to sign papers at every step of the sale process. Then came the logistics of packing up and emptying the house of anything that could not be taken to India. My mother's dementia had not deteriorated to the point where she could not make decisions about what she could or could not take with her. She was lucid enough to know that some things meant more to her than others, and to whom she wished to give some of her possessions. I was stunned at how many clothes and things my mother had hoarded over the years. Packing became a source of stress when she insisted on keeping things for which there was no storage space at the home in India. Even though she eventually relented, it was heart-breaking to enforce a strict, needs-based criteria for what she could take with her. By the time we had packed all the things my mother would need, we had more than three decades of my mother's life packed into just two 28-inch suitcases. I had eliminated a large chunk of things associated with her life from all those years – from her first move to Washington, where she had worked at Boeing, and 12 years later, her retirement to

California – and wondered if I should have saved more. It was too late. I convinced myself that it would not be long before the things would no longer mean anything to her, and that she would not be able to associate a memory to them. To be sure she had at least a few familiar things, I packed some framed photographs of our family and a few relatives, a bedspread she particularly liked (which I thought was drab and rather ugly), the mug which she used for her tea, and two glass jars for the almonds and walnuts which she took daily.

Immediately after the city council approved the buyer's application, I booked our flights to India, with a one-week stopover in Singapore. By now, I was utterly exhausted and homesick. I missed my family and the comforts of my home. My mother was keen to see her friends for what we all knew was going to be her last time. We had only four days to our departure and too many farewell lunches and dinners to attend. My mother was tired and disoriented, but managed to be composed throughout. I, on the other hand, was exhausted and did not wish to see anyone, which, unfortunately, was not an option as I could not dishonour my mother, nor disrespect her friends.

We were due to leave on a Monday night. There was still a lot of sorting to do – things to be given away, or kept by me, or, if they had to be thrown away, then I had to do it by the next night, in time for collection by the weekly recycling truck the following morning. I could not afford to miss that time slot and leave a pile of rubbish for the new owner. By nine o'clock that night, I had eight large garbage bags filled with things we could neither take nor give away, mostly photo albums, documents in files, cards and letters, and old towels and sheets. I lugged them to my mother's recycling bin, which I had wheeled out to the pavement earlier that evening for the waste collection the next day, but it was soon close to overflowing with the additional two oversized bags. Her friends within the development kindly agreed to let me place the rest of the bags in their bins.

Just as I had dumped the last bag into a bin, I leant forward, trembling and unable to breathe. I fell to my knees and buried my face in my hands, trying to breathe as deeply as I could. It took a few minutes before I recognised it as a panic attack. I do not remember for how long I had sat on the pavement, but, as I walked back to my mother's house, I saw a car turning into the street I was on. At the spur of the moment, I wanted to jump in front of it. I immediately realised that the car was going too slowly to kill me. Besides, the driver slowed down when he saw me, and stopped to let me cross. I thanked him and chided myself for such a stupid thought. The responsibility for getting my mother the care she truly deserved now rested entirely on my shoulders, and for that, I needed to be alive.

That night, when it hit me hard that I was now entirely responsible for my mother's well-being, I was filled with fear and anxiety. I did not think I was up to it. I watched my mother, sleeping peacefully, without a care in the world, and I wept. The next morning, I promised her that I would ensure she received the best care in India, and that I would visit her often. For the first time since I arrived in California, she laughed and said that was a good reason for her to go to India.

I knew that no matter how I felt, no matter how close to the precipice I found myself, I had to stay alive. I knew I could expect many challenges to present themselves, and, somehow, I had to overcome them. Our journey had just begun and I was not sure I had the strength.

Throughout our one-week stopover in Singapore, my mother was calm, but sad. Several times she asked if she could live with me, instead of moving to India. Each time, I said, I'm afraid not, Mummy, I am physically and mentally incapable of looking after you. Her response was always the same: but I can take care of myself, I won't give you any trouble. I wish that had been true, but even so, I still feel remorseful for not making any effort to accommodate my mother. At the same time, I knew then that I could never have coped with the demands of taking care of my mother, certainly not when she had Alzheimer's disease.

The night before we left for Mumbai, my mother seemed resigned to leaving her old lives behind – her childhood in pre-partition India (now Pakistan), her teenage and young adult years in India, 27 years in Singapore, followed by 32 years in America – never to return to Singapore or America. On the drive to the airport, she seemed wistful, but when I reminded her that she would be living close to her old home, Bombay (I used the old name, as my mother could not remember that the city had changed its name and was now called Mumbai), she smiled and said, I'll see Dada and Ami, referring to her late parents. Yes, I said, knowing she would forget by the time we got to the airport. I sensed that a part of her was keen to return to the country of her birth.

The flight to Mumbai was uneventful. I watched two movies, while my mother alternated between sleeping and staring at the ceiling. Every now and then, I asked her if she needed anything. No, she said, shaking her head. She seemed sad, but I did not know what to say to comfort her. The five-hour-long flight felt like an eternity.

As we emerged from the departure hall and headed towards the car which we had pre-booked, my mother perked up a little. This is Bombay, she asked. Yes, Mummy, once upon a time, your home. Long ago, she said. We got into the car, and she faced the window throughout most of the two-hour drive. She had been up since four o'clock that morning, and I could tell she was tired. The first half of the drive from the airport was unbearable for me. The air-conditioning in the car did not work, so we had to wind down the windows, which was not a problem as it was a cool morning. It was the relentless honking from what felt like a thousand cars around me that gave me an evil headache.

We arrived at the home in the early afternoon. I helped my mother onto her small wheeler towards the lift, while the male staff helped with the bags. As I left my mother near the lift, I went back to check that all the bags had been unloaded. Walking down the corridor once again, I had the same sinking feeling just minutes earlier, when I first walked into the home. It was depressing. The place was most displeasing: the long corridor was tiled with large, shiny slippery tiles, which ran through the entire home, increasing the possibility of falls amongst the elderly residents; the walls were filthy, and spiders had spun their cobwebs in almost every corner, safe in the knowledge that they would not be destroyed; mosquitoes flew around happily, though not always on a feeding frenzy, and worst of all, the lift did not work and we were told that it could take several days for it to be repaired.

I helped my mother up four flights of stairs to get to her room, stopping at every landing for her to rest her legs. I was keen for my mother to assimilate into her new environment; to have conversations; to make new friends; to be more sociable, and all these were only possible if she could get from the third floor to the dining room and corridor on the ground floor. Without a lift and with her weak legs, it would be an ordeal for her, even if we limited such socialising to one meal a day.

As we entered the room, I walked my mother to the edge of the large bed, sat her down, and introduced her to her new home. She looked at me, shook her head and began to cry. No, no, this is not my home. Please take me back to America. Please, please take me to my real home, she begged. I held her close and said that she would have to live here from then on because she needed full-time care. No, no, no, she protested, I want to go. Let me die, right now, you must help me. Stunned, I stared at my mother. For the first time in my life, I saw the desperation in the eyes of someone who had given up on life, who wanted nothing more than to die. Instantly, I wondered if those were the eyes I would have seen had I bothered to look in the mirror during my darkest moments, when death beckoned. I looked away. No, Mummy, I said softly. I cannot, and will not, help you. I asked her to lie down while I put our three suitcases in a corner and went to get us some lunch. My mother hardly ate, but she had a nap and soon after waking up, she felt better, but she was still disoriented.

I pointed out how lovely her space was: her room on the top floor was bright and airy, with floor-length windows on one side and tall windows on another, looking out to coconut palms, swaying in the gentle breeze. The views of the Western Ghats in the distance, even when shrouded in a polluted mist, would be a welcome sight every morning. She smiled for the first time since we left Singapore that morning. While the room was bright, spacious and comfortable, and was quite possibly the nicest room she had ever lived in, the home itself was dinghy and depressing. There were between 15 and 18 residents, mostly women, varying in age between early 60s and 90s. The staff comprised two live-out cleaners, and two live-in staff, a cook and his assistant who also served as the home's errand boy. None of the staff spoke English, and I could not speak Hindi, though I understood a few words. If I needed anything done for my mother, I had to call the owner-manager who lived more than two hours away in Mumbai, and had his own business to run. He assured me he was always in touch with the cook, and that I could call him at any time. While he meant to be helpful, I found his arrangement inconvenient and annoying.

In all my travels, whenever I had to deal with the systems of a foreign country, I would always be grateful for Singapore's efficiency, and rarely ever made comparisons. But India was something else altogether. Opening a bank account, with all my documents on hand, took three hours. The three-page carbon forms had to be filled in using a fine-point ballpen. After two hours of waiting for the forms to be filled, I was starting to get hungry and irritable. I was asked to provide a utilities bill with my name and my address. The bank officer insisted that it had to be a utilities bill, not a credit card bill. I stood up and, in a voice loud enough for the customers and staff within that small room to hear, I asked the bank officer if his utilities bill was in his wife's name. No, he said, before I turned to ask his colleague, and some random customers, if any of their household bills were in their wives' names. By now, I was shrieking. Everyone just stared at me. I stopped within a minute or two, when I could not even bear the sound of my own voice. Alright then, the bank official said, your credit card statement will do. I sat down, bursting into tears as I called the bank in Singapore to send me my statements from the past three months. The bank manager apologised. Rules, madam, he said. I sulked. The whole process was over in three hours, by which time I was famished and exhausted. Just before I left, the bank manager came to the cubicle and apologised for the delay. He was most solicitous, at which point I felt ashamed for my outburst and apologised profusely to the manager, the officer and the staff.

After that incident at the bank, I tried to lower my expectations of how things worked in India, whether I found myself in a big, modern city like Mumbai, one of the world's top 10 largest cities, or in a small, conservative village where my mother was.

By the fourth day, I was already quite distressed with the lack of a support system for my mother, and was beginning to believe that I had made the wrong decision. I researched alternative homes within a two-hour drive from Mumbai, so her friends and relatives could still visit her. None of them worked for various reasons, ranging from shared rooms to not allowing personal, full-time caregivers. I resigned myself to keeping my mother at this home, and making it work. It was after all, a lovely room, where she would spend most of her time, with a living and dining room on the same floor, which, in the absence of other residents on the same floor, she had all to herself.

Hard as it was, I tried to be as calm as possible around my mother, but there were times when I would forget, and would lash out at the staff, or well-meaning residents who all offered unsolicited advice, or on the phone with the manager, and worst of all, at my mother. Even when I was calm, my mother would sense my vexation, and apologise. I wish I could just go, right now, she would say nearly every day. I always replied, please don't say that. I am only trying to ensure your comfort and welfare are taken care of. I reminded her that I did not have a good mind, that I was, in fact, unwell. I did not tell her that all this stress had made me more manic, and that I had deliberately avoided the anti-psychotic pills so I could be lucid during every waking moment while I was with her. I also needed the energy to run errands in the old town 10 kilometres away.

Without the pills, my mind raced like a chicken running for its life. Late one moonlit night, when stillness had descended upon the home, I lay in bed and heard my mother's light breathing. I was exhausted, but could not sleep for thinking of all the things I had to do the next day. Staring at the fan, whirring just enough to keep the mosquitoes away, I toyed with the idea of hanging myself with the thin bedsheet under which I lay. I turned to look at my mother, and immediately admonished myself for even thinking I could leave her at a time when she needed me most. But she's safe in this home, and, unlike a few residents who did not have relatives responsible for their existence, my husband and children would help with facilitating monthly payments and making decisions about her medical needs. These thoughts drained me, and soon, I fell asleep.

Three days before I left – I had already been there for 10 days – the manager confirmed that he had found a caregiver, a woman in her 60s who had worked for his own family for more than 30 years. She arrived the evening before I left. My mother was suspicious at first, but I explained to my mother that the caregiver would be looking after her, and that I would continue to call my mother twice a day, every day, from Singapore. By the time I left my mother to return to Singapore, I had spent most of my time in the past six weeks with her. The last time I had spent that much time with her must have been when I was in pre-university. On the drive to the airport, I felt an agonising mix of relief, guilt, pain and longing, all woven into a tight knot in my heart. I wept on and off all the way to the airport, and on the flight home.

Never did I imagine being so frazzled by a place and its people, and yet be so grateful at the same time. The daily chaos, along with the noise, dust and smells drained me, but the gentleness and kindness of the people, even as I tried to suppress my frustration at their ineptitude, helped to get me through those gruelling days. It was a stark contrast to the ever-present efficiency, though often accompanied by coldness, that I had grown accustomed to in Singapore. Considering how easily enraged I became in India, I learnt to be thankful for how easy it was to get things done at home, never mind that sometimes people were grumpy or icy.

In the six weeks I had been away, sorting out my mother's move, I had lost over two kilograms, and probably a chunk of my soul. One of the first things I did when I returned home was to see my doctor at IMH. He was surprised at what I had gone through, saying that it was quite a feat for normal people, which made what I had done, and survived, that much more remarkable. He said that, despite the numerous meltdowns I had experienced, and the help I had received from my aunt and an uncle in California, I should be proud of myself for my fortitude in managing and organising my mother's new chapter from the moment I landed in America until my return home from India. As someone who finds it very difficult to take credit for anything, I found myself accepting and basking in all the affirmation from the one person who was responsible for treating my mental illness. He also prescribed a new dosage of 1000mg of lithium and more quetiapine. I did not question the additional dosage, knowing I needed stability now more than ever.

That evening, I told my husband and daughter what the doctor had said, and proclaimed the past six weeks as my greatest achievement. From then on, I told myself that every time I walked away from attempting suicide, or even thinking about it, that would be an even greater achievement.

Months later, when my mother had settled into her new environment, and I had continued to visit her in India, the reality hit me – I really did not care about achievements. As long as I felt the urge to die, it was only a matter of whether or not I succumbed to it. Achievements be damned.

Chapter 14

In recent years, there has been much discussion in Singapore about discrimination against the mentally ill, specifically in relation to employment. I was fortunate that, despite knowing about my mental health, I was employed by a woman who focussed on my ability to do the job. What I had never anticipated was discrimination for medical insurance. When my husband's employment with Singapore Airlines ended, so did our medical insurance. We now needed a plan to cover us for the rest of our lives.

The Integrated Plan launched by the Ministry of Health in partnership with Central Provident Fund seemed like the ideal plan. We contacted the five agencies offering the plan and we made an appointment with an agent who had responded promptly. She explained the details of the various plans, and we agreed on her recommendation. We filled in the forms, and she assured my husband that his application will be approved but mine would be a problem because of my bipolar disorder diagnosis. My husband pointed out that my mental condition has no bearing on the illnesses for which we were seeking coverage.

We told the agent that if I were a smoker or heavy drinker – I was neither – I should be flatly rejected as a liability, yet Prudential would approve my application. The agent said she would check with her underwriter and get back to me. Two days later, she called to say that my application had been rejected on account of my mental condition.

I tried all the other agencies which offered the Integrated Plan. At that time there were five – AIA, Aviva, Great Eastern, NTUC Income and Prudential. I was rejected by all of them. Great Eastern told me not to bother applying because my application would definitely be rejected.

Disheartened, I pointed out that I was fit and healthy. I exercised regularly and was careful about what I ate. More importantly, I was neither a smoker nor a drinker. But the answers were the same – not approved. All because I had a mental disorder. I mentioned to every agent that I was being rejected for something I had in common with some people they might have heard of, and threw in several names – Catherine Zeta-Jones, Graham Greene, Winston Churchill, Nina Simone, Lee Joon, Demi Lovato, Carrie Fisher and Eason Chan. The list went on: Mel Gibson, Stephen Fry, Edgar Allan Poe, Abraham Lincoln, Virginia Woolf, Ernest Hemingway, Amy Winehouse, Vincent Van Gogh, Friedrich Nietzsche, Ludwig van Beethoven, Charles Dickens, Isaac Newton, Florence Nightingale. The list did go on but I stopped after rattling off at least six names, making sure I always mentioned Dickens and Beethoven. It did not matter to the agents and their underwriters that these people were amongst the greatest artists, musicians, performers, writers and thinkers who ever lived. I told them that I could not, and dared not, compare myself to any of these leaders in their respective fields, but, great as their achievements were, they were also, first and foremost, people. Just like me, and like about 2 per cent of the world's population, including Singapore's. People with bipolar disorder.

When I appealed to the insurance companies, I provided them with a doctor's report from the Institute of Mental Health, which stated that I was compliant with medication and in full recovery. I stressed that with diligent medication and visits to the doctor, I am able to function as normally as anyone.

Still, my appeals were rejected. I questioned the discrimination – after all, they could simply provide exclusions for any psychiatric treatment or injuries arising from my condition, for instance, injuries sustained in a failed suicide attempt. Some of the agencies raised the issue of two other minor and common ailments but when challenged, agreed that without bipolar disorder, I would get an IP with exclusions for those ailments. The rejection was blamed squarely on bipolar disorder.

Discrimination forces people to keep fighting for equitable treatment. So, on a friend's advice, I went to see my Member of Parliament at a Meet-the-People Session armed with an appeal letter, along with all the rejection letters. I did not get to meet my MP but his team of volunteers who looked into my case were very helpful. They said it was unlikely that any of the international agencies would bother about a letter from an MP, and advised focusing on NTUC Income as it was my best chance. I left feeling hopeful because my MP was none other than Minister Chan Chun Sing.

Several weeks later, I received a letter from NTUC Income, which said this, after the usual official "courtesies":

"We hope you understand that it is our duty to underwrite each case according to our underwriting guidelines consistently so as to be fair to the others who contribute to the risk pool."

I was disappointed but had to laugh at the absurdity of the mention of "risk pool", wondering how I could be at a greater risk than someone who drank and smoked heavily and who may even be obese. Risk of what, exactly, I asked out loud. The letter ended with this:

"Moving forward, we are willing to assess your coverage in future, when you have fully recovered and have been discharged from your follow up for your bipolar disorder condition without the need for medication."

I did not know whether to laugh or cry. The person who had written the letter obviously had no idea that the day I am discharged from my follow-up, when I no longer need medication, will be the day I die. Bipolar disorder is incurable. What was even more absurd was that it came from NTUC Income, a company which had featured me on their first Future Peek campaign. They had no qualms about using an intimate account of my experience as a bipolar disorder patient for marketing and to sell their policies, yet spat me out without hesitation when I wanted to buy an Integrated Plan. NTUC Income's website at that time made this claim –

"Insurance Made Simple, Made Honest, Made Different" and with great emphasis, "People. First". To me, they were empty promises written by a copywriter at an advertising agency. The spectacular hypocrisy of a large national organisation which claims to "make essential insurance accessible to all", left me feeling discouraged about the end of discrimination against mental health conditions in Singapore. I wondered, if I could bring Isaac Newton, Beethoven or Charles Dickens back to this future, living in Singapore and requiring an Integrated Plan, would these insurance agencies deny them coverage? I could not help but think, yes, absolutely, in a heartbeat.

Mental illness has no known comorbidity with physical illness. By rejecting my application and appeals, these insurance companies deliberately denied me coverage for illnesses such as cancer, heart disease and diabetes, all of which have no relation to my mental state.

I made a random check with the overseas offices of three of the international insurance agencies which had rejected my application – Prudential, AXA and AIA. All three agencies offered critical illness plans for psychiatric patients, though with exclusions. Some plans offered supplementary coverage for psychiatric care. When I asked about their policy of discrimination in Singapore, all agencies I had spoken to said that they left it to local offices to create policies as required. Essentially, there was no justification for the discrimination, and agencies could get away with such behaviour in Singapore because there was no law against it.

Discrimination against people with a mental health condition is very real in Singapore, cutting across all areas. In a survey conducted by the National Council of Social Services in 2018,[1] it was found that:

- 5 in 10 people believe that people with a mental health condition should not be given any responsibility.
- 6 in 10 believe that mental health conditions are caused by lack of self-discipline and willpower.
- 7 in 10 believe that people with mental health conditions experience stigma and discrimination in their daily lives.
- 8 in 10 believe that being part of the community is therapeutic for people with mental health disorders.
- 9 in 10 believe that the community needs to be more tolerant towards those with mental health issues.

More than half are not willing to live with, or close to, or work with, a person with a mental health condition.

I was utterly dismayed by this report, which was released at the launch of "Beyond the Label", a five-year public education campaign to combat stigma against mental illness. In a country where the number of people seeking help for mental health issues has risen, especially during the pandemic, it would be a tragedy if more people were avoiding help because of the attitudes reflected in this report. With death rates from suicide being notoriously high for people with a mental illness, this could mean needless deaths due to society's discrimination against a particularly vulnerable group.

As a pioneer mental health advocate at the Institute of Mental Health (IMH), I was invited to the launch of the campaign at the Mental Health Festival, organized by IMH. I listened

---

1   National Council of Social Services www.ncss.gov.sg Press Room, Press Release NCSS Launches First Nation-Wide Campaign to Fight Mental Health Stigma

keenly as the guest of honour, Deputy Prime Minister Tharman Shanmugaratnam, spoke in his usual calm, engaging and articulate manner. When he said that he hoped the campaign will show that persons with mental health disorders can be active contributors to society, and urged Singaporeans to include those with mental health conditions in society, rather than shut them out, I tried to share the same hope. It has been two years since much publicity surrounded the campaign. Ingrained negative perceptions take time to change, and I am not entirely hopeful that a new report five years after the last one will show an improvement.

With much optimism, I look forward to the day when it will be unlawful for insurance companies to deny medical insurance to anyone with a mental disorder. Just like everyone else, we will grow old and might need coverage for critical illness. Legislation will be one major step towards eliminating discrimination against the mentally ill.

Chapter 15

A few months after my husband had left for Ethiopia, a domestic helper who had worked with us for 14 years, decided to retire. There was not much for her to do, and after nearly 30 years in Singapore, she felt it was time to be with her ageing parents. I was very sad to see her go, and decided that I would not hire a replacement, and instead try to manage without a domestic helper. I liked the freedom, and felt capable of taking care of myself and my home with the help of a part-time cleaner twice a week.

Within a few months, I started to feel as if I might have taken on too much, but, at the same time, tried to deny that I was incapable of managing without a full-time domestic helper. After all, I was alone most of the time, a part-time domestic helper came in to clean once or twice a week, and when my husband was home, there were only three of us to cook for. But that was precisely the problem – while there was not much to do in the three weeks my husband was away, the 10 days during which he was home was quite hectic. I found it hard to make the transition from doing as I pleased and when I pleased, to scheduling my days around my husband. He never asked for much, never even expected to be fussed over, but after three weeks in Ethiopia, flying to cities in Africa, China and Europe, subsisting on airline and hotel food, all he craved was home-cooked meals when he returned. That was easy for me, as I love cooking, and get much pleasure out of cooking for my family. But I soon got tired of the other activities that accompanied cooking – the planning, the shopping for ingredients, the preparation and the washing up – no matter how simple the food was.

Within two years, I had hired four domestic helpers, with intervals of up to six months in between, none of whom were suitable. I always made it very clear at interviews that I was obsessive about cleanliness and hygiene, which meant that some chores had to be done a certain way. They all assured me it would not be a problem. But it was always a problem. One, who confessed to being particularly troubled by debt from illegal loans and could not focus on her work, cleaning the flat only when she felt like it, lasted barely a week. Another, who lacked basic intelligence, yet came highly recommended by a neighbour, lasted six weeks. The longest lasted six months. By the time she left, I was done with hiring another domestic helper.

It was during one of those intervals, when I did not have a domestic helper, that I felt utterly submerged on one of my husband's visits home. Up until then, I had run the household and done my housewifely chores while feeling relatively stable. It was not as if I woke up every morning looking forward to a day of cooking, cleaning and doing laundry, but I did not resist it either. I merely faced it with indifference. But one day, soon after my husband had returned home, I began to feel an irrepressible fear of being unable to cope with the chores. I could not think of what to cook for dinner, not for that night, nor for the next few days. While my husband was in his study, busy catching up with mail and other matters, I went to the domestic helper's room and sobbed. I could not let my husband see me like that, and not wanting to worry him, I took a few deep breaths, forced myself to focus on being a dutiful housewife and mother, and told myself that everything will be alright. Just like it always was. That night, I took an anti-psychotic to help me sleep and calm my mind for the next day.

A few days later, after the preparation of several lunches and dinners, and in the middle of my husband's visit home, the feeling of helplessness became so intense that I was afraid to step onto the balcony, fearing I would succumb to the urge to jump. My husband noticed my hesitation and asked what was wrong. I burst into tears and told him that I could no longer cope with caring for the family, and that I was feeling suicidal. He got out of his chair, held me close and said, you need to see your doctor, and promptly drove me to the hospital for an emergency appointment with my doctor, who yet again, was waiting for me after consultation hours had ended.

I told my doctor what I had omitted to tell him on my regular visits while my husband was in Ethiopia. In the few days since my husband had come home, I had alternated between feeling happy and sad, anxious and carefree, confident and incapable, and that I was drowning in these numerous and conflicting emotions. I had not known what to do and suicide seemed like an attractive option. These roller-coaster feelings had gone on for more than six months, but I had not said anything to him, fearing he would recommend a hospital stay, or worse, electroconvulsive therapy, something I could not bear to go through again. I told my doctor how one evening I was capable of making a wonderful meal, and barely 12 hours later, I fussed over a sandwich filling for lunch, convinced that the meal was going to be insipid. He heard more about my erratic week – one day I was happy to run errands with my husband, and the next day I fretted at the suggestion of going for a family walk at Marina Bay. During those four or five days, I had found it difficult to sleep and sometimes woke up with a start, unable to breathe.

My doctor, who was one of two of the best doctors I had seen in 12 years of being treated for bipolar disorder, recommended lorazepam, a strong drug used to treat anxiety. I thanked him profusely, having expected to be treated with shock therapy. Having been through the treatment once, I was determined to avoid the treatment again. Admittedly, ECT was very effective at the time I received it, but ever since then, whenever I had felt suicidal, my desire to die was always stronger than any innate need I had to remain alive. Somehow, it was always something or another, but not ECT, that prevented me from taking my own life. Nor was it the abhorrence of the treatment that prevented me from seeking effective help for preventing my suicide. It was precisely because I knew how effective ECT was, that I actively chose to avoid it if I was absolutely sure about suicide.

After an early dinner that evening, I took one dose of lorazepam. It knocked me out for 15 hours, and for two days, I barely left our room. My husband sorted out our meals and before I was completely well, his 10 days were up and he had to return to Ethiopia. I assured my husband that I was starting to feel much better, and expected to be back to my usual self within that week. He and our daughter had nothing to worry about, I promised.

After my husband had left for the airport, I had a light dinner, read a little and went back to sleep. For the next few days, I spent most of my time reading, trying to write and walking half-an-hour each way to hawker centres near me. As I had expected, I felt as good as I could possibly feel by the end of that week. But it only lasted for about six months.

Chapter 16

Between early 2015 and late 2020, I have had more suicidal ideation, both passive and active, worming its way through my head, with greater intensity and frequency, than I have ever had in my entire life. It was five years of upheaval interspersed with many joyful moments and magical holidays. With so many captivating sights and new experiences, those holidays kept me uplifted and close to my family. But life was never one long holiday; family and friends could only fill so many days with immense joy.

Within days of returning home and settling into my routine, I would feel carefree for a few weeks, and then I would return to the mundane task of running a home. Inevitably, something would crop up, something trivial, or more significant, that would throw me off-balance and once again, I would feel unable to cope with my situation and start thinking about an escape. Every now and then, my escape plan involved running off to Bali or Penang, and dying after several last meals and experiences, but such plans would only last for a few minutes, only to be replaced by thoughts of a more convenient death in Singapore.

Nothing quite prepared me for the responsibility of caring for my mother while she was at the old-age home in India. After that first trip, when I had placed her at the home and arranged for a caregiver to look after her, I visited her every three or four months, sometimes just a month later for appointments, for instance with the United States Consular Office or an important medical appointment, such as a visit to the neurologist.

After several visits, and not less than one meltdown each time, I found myself grappling with my inability to adapt to the Indian approach to anything and everything. The fact that the home did not have an in-house manager was a pet peeve about the home. There was no one to supervise the caregiver, who, despite being adequately competent, was stubborn and would do things her own way, regardless of whether or not it was good for my mother. Leaving my mother's care entirely to the caregiver left me in consternation throughout my mother's time there. Fortunately, the caregiver, who had about 70 days off a year, chose to accumulate the days by returning to her village for a few weeks every two months, and sending her daughter in her place, which also meant additional income for their household. It was an arrangement that worked perfectly, except that it came to a point where my mother much preferred the daughter, but we had to settle for the mother as the primary caregiver as there was no other option.

With the manager visiting once a week for only a couple of hours on a Sunday, and with a fleeting visit to each resident – never more than five minutes, and on some Sundays, he did not even visit my mother – all I could do was hope that my mother was receiving the care she deserved in my absence. My elderly aunt in Mumbai, who had recommended the home to my mother, visited her as often as she could, which was about once a month. My mother's friends from California also visited her when they were in Mumbai on their yearly visits.

Being miles away, I was forced to relinquish all control over my mother's care and treatment to the manager. His physical absence from the home, his lack of transparency with my mother's accounts, and what I perceived as his overall lack of professionalism, was always a huge source of stress for me. Having to get an assurance from him about the care I felt my mother deserved, was a far more daunting task than caring for my mother. I felt that he over-promised and under-delivered. Despite that, I knew that my mother was much better off in that home in India, than she would have been in any of the ones I had visited within a 20-mile radius of her home in California.

Even though my mother's dementia had advanced since her arrival in India, she would still be lucid enough to express a wish to die every now and then. I want to go, she would say. I would ask, Go where, Mummy? She would raise her arm, pointing towards the ceiling, and lament, go, you know, just go… but it is up to God… I don't know why he won't take me. Initially, I felt sad whenever she said such things, but after my third or fourth visit to India, when having to run errands, especially when going to the city in maddening traffic, I began to feel incapable of caring for my mother during the week I was there. It was better when I returned to Singapore but even then, on days when my mother was not feeling well, or was in one of her moods, I found it extremely stressful having to rely on the caregiver or the manager, never knowing whether or not their efforts were enough, and what I felt my mother deserved. Not being able to help my mother was sheer torture for me. Thankfully, those instances did not happen often, but when they did, passive suicidal ideation kicked in. Just as quickly, I would realise that my mother needed me, and I had to stay alive for her. Suicide was a comfort I could not even contemplate.

Chapter 17

In the middle of 2018, at the behest of my daughter and a friend, I signed up for yoga at a well-known studio. I had read and heard about yoga being beneficial therapy for anyone with a mental disorder. With my mind thrown in turmoil a little too often, and not keen on taking supplementary anti-psychotics, I signed up for 50 lessons, valid for a year. I started with an Iyengar class one Monday morning, and found myself in a class full of dedicated yoga practitioners who were adept at twisting and balancing their bodies and managed their poses with such grace and ease. I struggled with every pose, and ached as I reached to touch my toes with my fingers, only to find I had a very long way to go, while most of the other students could wrap their fingers around their toes, their arms rigid over their outstretched legs. By the end of the lesson, I knew I had to learn to enjoy yoga and to be patient before seeing, or feeling, the results. The next morning, my body ached all over. I could barely move, and was reminded of the time I had dengue fever just four years earlier. I cancelled the next day's lesson. After that, I went for classes regularly, allowing for longer breaks in between.

Towards the end of the year, I decided to try Pilates, and was hooked. I liked it more than yoga, but what I really liked was the small groups, and the few students who attended the same classes I did. When they saw me struggling, they would offer words of encouragement and tips for various moves.

It is true what the doctors and all the articles say concerning the management of bipolar disorder. Along with mood stabilisers, patients functioned best with these three components: 10 hours sleep at a stretch, a healthy diet with fruits and vegetables, and exercise. There was a noticeable difference in my mood when I managed all three in a matter of days, which explained why I did well on holidays. I felt stronger with Pilates, but not fitter. I then began to add 15 minutes, three times a week, on the elliptical machine which my husband had been using daily since he bought it several years ago. Within a few weeks, my regime comprised 30 minutes, five times a week. I was fitter, stronger, and felt more youthful. I went for weeks on end, feeling as close to normal as I had ever felt. I felt happy and hopeful. The noise from the neighbours upstairs had improved significantly, but there were occasions when it was still bad, jolting me out of a deep sleep. In general, there were now far more days in between when the noise was bearable – though still not ideal – and feeling better overall helped me cope. For the first time in years, I felt both physically and mentally fit.

A few months later, the early morning sounds resumed, but they were different – unlike the thumping, they were mostly from the children and woman having loud conversations in the bathroom. After having my sleep disrupted a few too many times, I ordered a pair of customised silicone ear plugs.

Combined with my new-found fitness, and the efficiency of the earplugs, I was able to sleep better, waking up later in the morning.

Chapter 18

When I visited my mother in January 2020, I was astonished by how much more frail she had become since the last time I had seen her, which was a mere three months earlier. Determined to see her more regularly, I told my mother that I was going on a winter holiday soon and that I had booked my next visit in April. I promised that thereafter, I would see her every two months. She was very happy, and so was I. On all my previous visits to my mother, I would leave with a leaden heart, but, at the same time, be glad to leave the chaos of one city for the predictability and efficiency of my home. On this particular visit, I had left with the same deep sadness, and had looked forward to returning soon.

Then, a virus, more wretched than any other in the last one hundred years, struck in early 2020.

Soon after I returned from visiting my mother in India, my husband and I began our winter holiday in America. Our daughters joined us on the eve of Chinese New Year in late January. The news in America focused on the dire situation in China and we read that the virus had reached our shores. At that time, America and Singapore had only one case each, both having travelled from Wuhan.

By the time we returned in early March from our holiday, the coronavirus was already starting to spread in parts of America and Europe; the relentless, deadly sweep across the world was still a month away. In Singapore, new cases were still in the low single digits, and there had not been any deaths reported from Covid-19. In India, when cases hit 500, Prime Minster Narendra Modi imposed a nationwide lockdown for 21 days, starting from 24th March. I immediately called my aunt and asked if it was possible for me to visit India as scheduled on the 21st of April, which was a few days after the proposed end date of the curfew. She said I should not count on it, as people were already expecting extensions on the lockdown. I continued to be optimistic and did not tell my mother anything about the possibility of not seeing her in April.

On 7th April, in Singapore, it became clear that the virus was spreading within the community, and that there was a risk of asymptomatic spread. In response, the government introduced a series of strict measures. In the days before the announcement, rumours were rife about food shortages. I believed them. The need to stock up on food and masks in the days affected me badly. My mind could not cope with a situation requiring me to plan for my family as if the apocalypse were imminent. My brain switched to succumbing to the wretched virus. I was more afraid of living with the restrictions brought on by Covid-19 than I was of the virus itself, despite reports at that time of painful deaths and even more painful recovery.

Collectively known as a circuit breaker, the measures included the closure of all non-essential workplaces, requiring thousands of people to work from home, while schools had to implement home-based learning. All food establishments – restaurants, cafes, hawker centres and kopitiams – could only provide take-away and delivery services. Even the Singapore Armed Forces was not spared; in-camp training and individual physical proficiency tests for operationally-ready NSmen were postponed until 4th May.

When the circuit breaker was announced, I immediately felt unsettled and insecure. My husband reminded me that in the prime minister's address to the nation, he had assured the public that markets and supermarkets would remain open for daily essentials, so we did not have to worry about not being able to buy food. But for me, it was not just about the food. It meant I had to limit my outings to protect my family, specifically, my older husband who was in the vulnerable age bracket. I could only go out when I needed to, masked and armed with hand sanitisers. My exercise routine, from which I had received much joy, had to be done at home.

The next night, I called my mother as usual. The caregiver had said that my mother had not been eating much in the past few days, and was sleeping a lot more than usual. My mother had seemed a little disoriented when I spoke to her that morning but I put it down to her having "one of those days", which, though rare, had happened before. That evening, she did not respond to anything I said. The caregiver said that my mother could not speak. My mind went racing. Something was very, very wrong. I asked the caregiver to call the manager. She said she had called him several times, but nothing had happened – there had not been a doctor, nor an ambulance, arriving at the home. I then called the manager and said that my mother might have had a stroke, and to please send a doctor to see her. The manager felt that my mother should go to the hospital instead, as doctors were not making house calls due to the number of patients they had to tend to at their clinics because of Covid-19 fears.

My mother had signed an advanced medical directive in America when she was in her late 50s, and again in her 80s, on top of making clear to me, that she would not want to be kept alive, and would much prefer to die at home. I asked the manager to keep my mother at home, in her room, on her bed, and to ask the caregiver and his staff to see to my mother's comfort. I also asked him to somehow find a doctor, and to pay him whatever he asked for, just to see my mother and tell me what was wrong.

It was nearly 1.30am – 11 o'clock at night in India – when a doctor arrived after his duty at a village hospital. The caregiver video-called me and immediately handed the phone to the elderly doctor. He told me my mother had suffered a stroke, and that she probably had two days left, maybe a few more, but unlikely. All the caregiver could do from then on was to keep my mother comfortable in her bed, and spoon-feed her some diluted milk every hour. There is nothing else, I'm afraid, said the doctor apologetically.

That night, while waiting for the doctor to visit my mother, I began looking for flights and options to get to Mumbai the next morning. All flights to India had been cancelled when India had announced the lockdown. With the country closed to foreigners, including those who, like me, carried special Overseas Citizens of India visas, there was no chance for us to travel to Mumbai. After speaking to the doctor, I sat in the dimly-lit living room, doing my best not to cry, while I struggled with the realisation that I would not see my mother again. I was at a loss, and in the still of the night, began to quietly curse the universe for denying me the opportunity to say goodbye to my mother. Realising that my rage only made me feel worse, I switched off the lamp on the side table, curled up on the sofa, and wept until I fell asleep.

The next morning, and for the next two days, I continued my daily calls, increasing the frequency to four times a day. I knew my mother was unconscious but I did not know whether or not she could hear my voice, or even recognise it. I had always been uncomfortable with saying those three over-used words, "I love you". To me, precisely because the phrase is so common, and while often used sincerely, it is also used routinely, even flippantly, which cheapened both the words and the sentiment. Until my late teens, I had only ever heard those words on English-language movies and television shows, and came to associate it with Western culture. I saw, and felt, more value in actions than words. I had grown up believing my Amah's love for me was absolute, and in my later years, after Amah had left us, I felt my mother's love. And from my 20s onwards, the love of my husband, children and friends have enriched me in ways that go far deeper and beyond those three pedestrian words. Yet, when making that first call to my mother after the news of her stroke, all I wanted to tell her was how much I loved her. She knew, of course, but I had not told her so in decades.

As my mother could no longer hold the phone, the caregiver had to put the phone to my mother's ear, as she had been doing for the past few days. I started with the usual hello, and even though I was not expecting a response, I choked when there was silence at the other end. Stammering at first, I said, in the most cheerful voice I could muster, who loves you, Mummy? I do! Lots! Sleep well, speak soon. Lots of love, big hugs, Mummy. Words, and variations of which, I repeated during every call, never knowing if she heard me, or even knew it was me speaking to her. I had hoped to let my mother know how much I loved her.

Just after sunrise on the morning of 11th April, I received a message from my aunt in Mumbai that my mother had passed away. She was 88 years old. A part of me was relieved that she did not suffer much, if at all, and that she had gone peacefully, which was something she had always hoped for. I just hope that when my time comes, I can go in my sleep, she would often say, whenever we spoke of someone's death. And she did. Even though I was mentally prepared for my mother's passing, which was imminent from the moment I had spoken to the doctor, I was inconsolable. I wondered if she heard me telling her how much I loved her: for two whole days, and a grand total of eight times. I would never know.

In keeping with Hindu customs, the manager of the home arranged for my mother's funeral to be held before sunset, in a nearby village. He had driven from Mumbai with my aunt and agreeably took on the duties of a son for the ritual. My aunt sent two short video clips of the cremation, which was remarkable in its simplicity. There was no coffin; my mother, dressed in a long batik dress, was lifted from an ambulance onto a bamboo stretcher, and transferred to a metal enclosure, which was lined with logs. Several more logs were then placed on top of my mother, after which someone poured oil from a large metal utensil. Just as someone else lit the log, my aunt stopped recording. I was thankful to not have witnessed my beloved mother being engulfed by flames. I replayed the video a couple of times that day, and found some peace in knowing that it was the kind of funeral my mother would have wanted – small and austere. It had all happened so quickly, barely 72 hours from the doctor's prognosis until the cremation. That evening, rather than dwell on my mother's death, I decided to honour her life. We had a vegetarian dinner and a glass of white wine, which was the only alcoholic drink my mother enjoyed, though she only drank it rarely.

Knowing how keen my mother had been to meet her maker, and had been since before she turned 80, I was happy for her. I kept telling myself that her departure was swift, peaceful and painless, as she would have wanted it, and that her funeral was exactly as she would have liked. She had also spent her last years in a home where she was comfortable and had all her needs catered to. Sometimes, relatives and friends visited her, and brought her much happiness. Her last years were as good as they could have ever been, and moving her to India was the best decision I could have made. As I tried to convince myself of all this, her friends and relatives said the same things, when I called them with news of my mother's death. But I simply could not overcome the guilt of not being there to bid her the farewell she deserved, to hold her close and to tell her how much I loved her and how much she meant to me. She knew this, of course, because she had always told her friends, how much I loved and cared for her.

I could barely eat, and spent a lot of time sleeping for the first week after my mother's death, and wept every now and then throughout the day. It did not help that I was housebound because of circuit breaker restrictions. I tried to read, and bake, and even to write, but I simply did not have the energy to even be distracted. Sometimes, I imagined I was talking to my mother, and I would tell her how much I hated my life, and that I would see her soon. Then I imagined her frowning and raising her voice slightly, saying, "You will do no such thing! You have a wonderful life. Live it!" Then, I smile, and say, okay, I won't join you just yet.

By the second week, stuck at home because of circuit breaker, I forced myself to continue doing what I enjoyed most – reading, writing and eating, not necessarily in that order. It was what my mother would have wanted, to get on with my life. What I did not expect was for the grief to be etched into my core. Although I was sleeping better, and had eased back into my daily routine, I still found myself, sometimes, doubling over, finding breathing to be arduous. I was having panic attacks and anxiety over my mother's death. After one of these attacks, which usually lasted less than five minutes – no more than 10 – I realised that, in my grief, numbed by guilt and sadness, I did not once think of suicide. Just as I was processing that thought in my mind, I felt a sense of relief. Immediately, I buried my face in my hands and tried to shake off the relief. It was regrettable, but at the same time, undeniable. It's okay,

I told myself. Mummy has been wanting to go for years. It was time for her. It's okay, I convinced myself. As I wept, I accepted the relief and, along with it, the freedom to commit suicide if ever I felt I had to.

Chapter 19

Based on early research by Dr. Edwin Shneidman,[1] doctors believe that acute suicidal crisis – that phase of high and dangerous lethality – is an interval of relatively short duration, which means that suicide as a transient state lasts typically hours or days, and not months or years. Within those hours or days, a suicidal person is either helped, changes their mind, or is found dead.

In an episode of the television series, *Parts Unknown*, Anthony Bourdain spoke of his struggle with depression. "*Welcome to the dark crannies of my skull,*" he said, as he was filmed visiting a therapist in Buenos Aires. He tells the therapist of how an episode of depression can be so easily triggered. "*I will find myself in an airport, for instance, and I'll order an airport hamburger. It's an insignificant thing, it's a small thing, it's a hamburger, but it's not a good one. Suddenly, I look at the hamburger and I find myself in a spiral of depression that can last for days.*" This was in 2016. Two years later, in 2018, Bourdain was found dead.

---

1   Shneidman ES, 1980. *Death: Current Perspectives, 2nd Edition.* Mayfield Publishing Company.

After my first attempt, when I had promised my husband that I would not make another attempt, I had become more aware of my acute suicidal phase. I have spent most of my life being non-suicidal, but during those times when I have been suicidal, the phase had lasted for about 10 minutes to two or three days. When I am in that phase, my awareness is heightened. When the duration is particularly short, I am either helped – an emergency visit to my doctor at IMH, for instance – or I cool off. Usually, I take a deep breath, or walk away from the situation that led me to have this urge in the first place, or I cry – often all at the same time – and soon after, the urge dissipates. For me to be able to prevent my own suicide, my mind needs to be lucid, to allow me to remind myself that I am not supposed to commit suicide, and to think of the consequences of my suicide. It is only then that I can pull myself back.

What I fear is what I cannot know, and cannot foresee – the possibility of an impulsive suicide. This has happened several times – when something happens to cause me unendurable anguish, and the world feels like it is whirling like a cyclone ready to sweep through and destroy the essence of my very being, when I become desperate for calm in my mind. Suicide is my obvious, my only, solution. Death is my salvation. I do not, I cannot, think about anything else, and certainly not about the family I am going to leave behind. Like that time when I had been sleep-deprived and had come to the point where I could no longer bear the noise from the neighbours upstairs. When I had wheeled the gas tank towards the kitchen, I had focused purely on killing myself. By the time the delivery man had left, I had decided not to proceed. On that day, I had been both, inadvertently helped, and in the intervening time, cooled off. Had it not been for the interruption by the delivery man, I might have died that afternoon.

Nearly every time I have considered suicide, or gone close to committing suicide, it was as a result of feeling utter desperation, sometimes combined with self-loathing, especially when I have been obnoxious and unkind towards others. After screaming at a shopkeeper in India for packing and charging me sweets I did not order, and seeing the dread on the face of every customer and employee, I left the shop, trembling as I got into a taxi. Within that hour, I would replay that scene, and hundreds of other similar scenes over the years, and think to myself, this is not the life I want to live, this is not the person I want to be. Just like that, while I reflected on my frightful behaviour towards strangers, suicide weaves its way into my mind, and becomes a very tempting solution.

This is how it has always been. Being on mood stabilisers has helped tremendously, but it was never the remedy I had hoped it would be. When I had first been diagnosed with bipolar disorder, and given medication which the doctor had said would help me function "more normally", I had been hopeful. I tried various medications and even doctor-hopped until I found a doctor whom I trusted unequivocally, and followed my medication regime diligently. I had believed that with medication, along with the side effects I had to endure, I would be stable all the time. None of the doctors had promised this, of course, but it was a foregone conclusion for me.

Yet, I had lapses. My episodes, mostly manic and rarely depressive, were fewer, and much less frequent than before my diagnosis. They were always a result of a trigger, typically unforeseen. It took my first manic episode while I was adequately medicated, to learn that even though my mood was now generally stable, a lapse and its severity would always be a possibility depending on the trigger. That also meant that my suicidal thoughts would never go away.

Chapter 20

Starting in March 2020, I saw my doctor as often as once a month. Never had I felt more suicidal, more frequently, than I had been in the months between March and August. It was during this time that I came to understand how little it took for me to be contented, and at the same time, how easily I was given to anguish. In the days before the announcement of Phase 1 of the circuit breaker, when it became possible to dine out once again, I made a list of people I was keen to see. The various small circles of friends, both old and new, with whom I had been socialising in the years before circuit breaker, were on top of the list. I then thought about friends and acquaintances whom I had not seen in over a year, and more, and drew up another list. I then remembered why I had not seen some of the people on this second list for several years, and promptly removed their names.

In the early months of my diagnosis, when I would sometimes see a counsellor, I had learnt the concept of boundaries. I was taught to know my limits and to set the emotional equivalent of a "no trespassing" sign for the protection of my mental health, which, for me, also meant self-preservation. I have never asked for, nor ever expected, preferential treatment or dispensations for my condition. If anyone had to compromise, it was me. As a result, I learnt that boundaries were essential for my survival.

Other than people, boundaries also included places and situations. After moving to Siglap, I found myself taking public transport more often, as I did not like driving to the city. While the bus or the train were my preferred choices, I sometimes took taxis, which, at least half the time, resulted in pleasurable rides with good and polite drivers, to whom I readily showed my appreciation. The rest of the time, there were too many taxis which smelt strongly of cigarettes or food, and when I mentioned it, the drivers would blame it on a previous passenger who reeked of smoke, something I found hard to believe. Every time this happened, I would wind the windows down for ventilation but most drivers objected to this. There were also drivers that would take a longer route when they realised I was distracted on the phone or reading a book. When I asked them about the unnecessary detour, they would make some excuse and immediately offer a discount. These instances caused me too much stress, and while it never became an episode of manic rage, it made me feel angry and helpless. I stopped taking taxis for nearly six months, until it became impractical to avoid them entirely, after which I decided to continue taking taxis but would leave soon after shutting the door if it smelt bad, or if the driver was grumpy, and pay the basic fare on the meter. The advent of private hire vehicles, with their rating systems, has provided options, but with the boundaries I set years ago, I still take taxis every now and then.

As for boundaries with people, I have, over the years, severed ties with friends from my childhood, and seen less of friends with whom I was once close. I stopped making plans with people who were habitually late. Even amongst close friends, I minimised the time I spent with those who drained me – a few expected more out of me than I was able, or willing, to give, or who had a transactional approach to friendship, whilst some had oversized personalities, and I could not feel calm if I spent more than a few hours in their presence. I would never dream of ending my ties with these friends, all of whom have always been extremely kind and thoughtful towards me. But I had to find ways to protect myself, and our friendship: by setting boundaries, which were flexible and relatively easy to set. For instance, I could spend a lot more time, even days, with these friends if we were part of a bigger group, reducing my one-on-one time with them. Far more difficult were the boundaries I had to set in certain situations, which had to be the equivalent of a high, inflexible, vertical wall that could neither be scaled nor demolished.

Recently, I severed ties with one of my oldest friends, someone I had known all my life. We had fallen out a couple of times in the last 30 years, but because I valued our long history of friendship, I invariably extended the olive branch. Each time, I knew I would soon regret it, and each time I did, but nevertheless, I tried to be more tolerant by focussing on our shared history. Until one incident made me realise that I had to erect that high, inflexible wall to protect myself.

It happened in late August 2020, and over an incident where I was doing her friend a favour, a friend I did not even know. In the course of a conversation, I felt she had used a contemptuous tone, with a facial expression to match. Shocked and agitated, I walked away. As I drove home, and thought about her response that morning – seemingly small, but enlarged by her expression – I began to cry. Her behaviour was typical, and it should not have affected me but it did, when I realised that I could not even remember the last time I had felt joyful from being in her company. I was now angry with myself, for allowing myself to be treated so dismally.

As soon as I reached home, I dumped my bag and keys on the floor and ran to my husband, sobbing. I need to get her out of my life, forever, no second chances! I am suicidal, I can't deal with this! Immediately, I regretted saying I was suicidal. I wasn't feeling it earlier, and it must have crept up on me as I reached home. My husband put his paper down, and gave me a hug. He knew immediately to whom I was referring. I told him what had happened. He asked me if I really was suicidal. I shook my head.

After ranting for a few minutes, I had a light breakfast, after which I blocked her on social media, email and my handphone. After six months of feeling fragile from circuit breaker, and several months of grieving over my mother, I had finally felt a new-found strength and a liberation that felt intoxicating. For the first time in months, I felt completely and utterly alive. All from abandoning nearly six decades of friendship, nearly half of which were onerous and hurtful.

While I put boundaries in place for some people, I strengthened ties with a number of friends and reconnected with old friends. At the same time, I kept myself surrounded within my usual, small circle who were always kind to me, people on whom I could always rely. A few of them pampered me, and often, too: picking me up and taking me out for a meal; sending me exquisite pies; sending me flowers, with a beautifully-made plush rabbit; inviting me over for a meal; calling me to say hello; and some did all of the above... With every gesture, I felt the strengthening bonds of friendship cultivated over love and respect.

To avoid imposing on my friends, I have never been one to call them when I needed cheering. I have never wanted to be in a situation where I am needy, and have to wear my friends down with my boring and tiresome company. But somehow, they are there, without having to ask. Without even making an effort, with only their absolute kindness, they, along with my husband and daughters, give me enough sustenance to stay alive.

Chapter 21

The restrictions on dining out affected me most about circuit breaker. It meant not being able to eat at a hawker centre or kopitiam. Ever since I started my working life as a stewardess with Singapore Airlines, the hawker centre experience has been an integral part of my life. Upon returning from overseas flights, I would go to a hawker centre for my fix of whatever it was that I missed while I was away. Top of my list was chicken rice, followed closely by mee pok tar, yong tau fu, and laksa. There were other favourites, too, but there were only so many meals I could have within the few days off I had between flights. When I had lived in Bali for two years, I would return home for a week every few months, and during those breaks, I would visit kopitiams and hawker centres near my home for lunch nearly every weekday. I would choose the places depending on what I felt like having that day. That often meant taking a bus to Bedok corner for satay or cheng tng, or to Old Airport Road for hokkien mee or prawn mee. Very soon, the hawker centre had become my lifeline.

Circuit breaker meant that I had to have my meal delivered, or picked up. Either way, I usually ended up with soggy noodles, which I found barely edible. I took to driving to the hawker centre, standing in line with my own utensils, and rushing back to the car to eat. The food, usually noodles – fishball noodles, char kway teow, hokkien mee, wantan mee, mee rebus – tasted much better in the car than they did at home, but still, not quite right. Then I realised, it was not only about the noodles. It was also the whole ritual of sitting at a familiar place and soaking up the atmosphere I had come to embrace as my place of safety and comfort. Whether it was hot and humid, or cool and breezy, and whether it was busy or relatively quiet, I had always felt a sense of satisfaction and belonging at a hawker centre. During circuit breaker, I felt a deep sense of loss and sadness seeing the tables and chairs taped to prevent anyone from sitting down.

It was during one of these days when, without thinking, I ordered takeaway laksa and tried to eat it in the car. It was impossible for me to hold the bowl and use both chopsticks and a spoon at the same time – I like my laksa when eaten from a spoon, using my chopsticks to place a few strands of the slippery white noodles onto a small pool of rich coconut gravy. I could not do that sitting in my car. All the sundry shops were closed, so I could not buy a tray on which to balance the bowl. I replaced the flimsy top on the disposable bowl of my laksa, brought it home, and forced myself to eat a few spoonfuls before throwing the rest away. I was very upset with the frequency at which I had thrown away some of my favourite foods in the past two weeks. I was even more upset that I could not eat at the hawker centre, even though I was thankful for being allowed out, unlike in some countries in a complete lockdown.

At that time, no one knew how long the circuit breaker would last. Weeks, months... there were rumours that Phase 2 would begin sometime in June or July, but no one knew when. The shops in the HDB estates were all closed, turning the once-vibrant neighbourhoods into lifeless spaces. I missed the banter of elderly uncles and aunties, especially when they spoke in dialect, taking me back to a Singapore that I liked to remember, before the Speak Mandarin Campaign extended its reach to the heartlands and gained ground in the mid-1980s. I missed chatting with the hawkers, who now kept communication to a minimum, and rightly so. I began to feel as lifeless as the places I visited. Not knowing when this would be over only made things harder for me.

One morning, as I shuffled from the market to my car, carrying a shopping tote in each hand, I crossed Holland Drive without looking. A car blared his horn, forcing me to step back towards the road divider. Stunned, having just missed being run down, I nodded an apology as the man in the car glared at me as he drove past, shaking his head. I had been so lost in my thoughts that I had not even considered my safety. Once I crossed the road, I turned back to look at the spot where, just moments ago, I had had a close shave with possibly a broken bone or two. I would not have died, as the car was not going quickly enough for a deadly impact, but I might have been hurt. As I turned around to walk to the car, I wished, just for a moment, that the car had been speeding, and I had been a split second quicker. That would have placed me right in front of the driver, who would have run me down and probably killed me. With the country feeling anything but alive, I wished, at that moment, that I had died.

A few weeks later, a friend baked me the most exquisite brownies, at a time when I was researching updated ideas for a painless suicide. She had no idea what I was going through, which made me treasure her gift that much more. All thoughts of suicide dissipated immediately. Augmented by similar acts of kindness by other friends in the weeks preceding my poorly state, and several happy outings with family in the following weeks, I did not think about suicide for nearly four months.

Chapter 22

After the late 2018 launch of my last novel, *It Happened On Scrabble Sunday*, I was hankering to write another crime story. I had some ideas, but was not confident that I could write a whole novel. I asked my husband for an idea, thinking I should try writing a novel around a crime committed by a pilot.

After we had brainstormed the plot and characters, I had believed I could start writing. By the time I had finished the first three chapters, I found myself stuck, unable to write another scenario or dialogue. Having written novels set in Singapore, with largely Asian characters, I was unable to create credible English, specifically "white people", characters and dialogue. Several months into struggling with the novel, I turned to my husband for help. We had gone as far as finalising a tightly-woven plot, created some credible characters and written at least 10 chapters, before we set aside the manuscript while travelling several times, up to two months each time. In between, we wrote a few chapters but, with all the distractions of planning holidays and the travelling itself, did not get much further.

It was only in early 2020, when we returned from our last vacation, during the early weeks of the coronavirus, that we focused on writing again. We started from the first chapter and made many significant revisions. By the time we reached where we had stopped a few months earlier, I felt my husband was capable of writing this novel himself. Having abandoned the idea of writing a plot-driven novel, on my own, I was keen to start writing my own literary novel, something in the contemporary women's genre. But my husband would only continue with this aviation crime novel if I worked on it with him, side by side.

Every afternoon, we would set aside about four hours to write, starting from 1.30pm until 5.30pm. Our collaboration started off well, but soon turned out to be extremely stressful for me. The plan was for my husband to dictate the lines, and I would type them. Along the way, I would offer my opinion on a scene, or dialogue, which usually led to a discussion. I enjoyed this and would happily participate. As we progressed, it was clear that the novel was a collaborative effort, that we both contributed equally, making the creative process equally rewarding for both of us. But it was the process that annoyed me, specifically my husband's insistence on reviewing the previous day's work before starting with the new work. I felt this slowed down the process, and became repetitive. To be fair, it was a disciplined approach to writing, where we were clear on the plot, making revisions where necessary, before moving on. But it was not how I worked; I usually wrote and thought up scenes and dialogues as I went along, allowing them to present themselves as I began typing the first words every day.

By the end of April, with the circuit breaker restrictions firmly in place, I was starting to feel suffocated. We had just finished writing the novel, and had started to edit it with a grammar programme we had purchased online. The instructions we found online seemed to offer a more specific and detailed editing programme, but the version we had purchased seemed more basic. I tried to find out why this was the case, while my husband, who was trying to help, was quite sure it was something I had or had not downloaded or installed properly. When he insisted I check again, I became increasingly agitated, and at one point, to a simple question my husband had asked in a kindly tone, I screamed, and swore, before continuing what I was doing just before that. I could not see that coming, but hours later, I still felt badly about the outburst.

From the next day onwards, it was a struggle to finish editing the manuscript. It took several more days, and once that was done, I spent my afternoons reading for several weeks in a row.

Throughout the process of writing and editing, between March and May, I experienced frequent mood swings, which were more intense than usual. We wrote in the living room, where we could cast our laptop screen onto the television screen. The noise from upstairs had gotten worse because the whole family was home all day, and the children ran and jumped just above us. We could not go anywhere else in our flat to escape the pounding above our heads. Early on several mornings, before 7 o'clock, the children would run into the master bedroom and have a conversation with the mother, who would speak in her loud voice, jolting us from our sleep every few days. This was on top of sounds in the middle of the night, where our neighbours would drop things on the floor, or drag furniture, or bang a door. My husband tolerated the noise, and I tried to do the same, only to find I was drained from the effort.

For anyone with a mental illness, sleep is crucial. All my doctors had recommended 10 hours, ideally. I was lucky if I got seven hours, which was rarely ever unbroken. Being sleep-deprived made me irritable, and being irritable reduced my ability to control my emotions, something which I was never very good at anyway. Combined with trying to process the grief from my mother's recent death, I felt perpetually exhausted. Within weeks, I was in despair, merely existing. Suicidal ideation weaved in and out of my mind nearly every other day, from minutes to hours, for several weeks. A few times, it lasted for more than a day, when passive suicidal ideation morphed into active suicidal ideation. Several times, I found myself having imaginary conversations with my late Amah and mother, telling them how much I missed them – I still grieve for my Amah more than 30 years after her death – and was looking forward to being reunited with them. The imaginary response was rebuke, but it was not enough to stop me from considering suicide. This was when I took quetiapine more regularly.

One morning, while I was in the kitchen trying to escape from a particularly bad episode of children thumping and stomping upstairs, I heard the condominium manager speaking to the woman about a complaint. The woman screamed at the manager, saying "F*** off! Tell them to deal with it!" I froze. I had not complained, and feared she assumed it was me. After five minutes, when I knew the manager would be back at her office, I called and begged her to tell the woman that it was not me. I explained that I could not handle even the most remote possibility of a retaliation from the woman.

When rumours began swirling about Phase 2 of circuit breaker, when it was possible to dine out again and resume exercising at the studio, I immediately felt hopeful. As soon as our prime minister announced the lowering of some restrictions, I cheered. The pervasive suicidal thoughts that had dominated my thoughts, on and off, for weeks, were now duly evicted.

I resumed my visits to the Pilates studio days after it re-opened during circuit breaker Phase 2 in mid-June, and, with four or five classes a week, I felt fitter by the end of that first month back, but I did not feel energised. The noise from upstairs had improved enough for me to sleep better, and thankfully, the jumping became less frequent.

On many languid afternoons, I spent my time indulging in one of my favourite activities – reading novels. I would only manage to finish 20 pages, having spent too much time re-reading sentences before anything sank in. Every now and then, I would also stop and stare at the ceiling, not thinking about anything, my mind a complete blank. This inability to focus is one of the symptoms of bipolar disorder, but it was an innocuous symptom and occurred every now and then. Being familiar with this symptom, and knowing it did not result in other symptoms appearing concurrently, I dismissed it.

Before and after reading a book, I would also surf the internet. As one of a few administrators on a local socio-political social media page, I would visit the page, either to participate in a discussion, or to monitor the comments and ensure that members were not breaching the rules. This was a welcome distraction for me, and, depending on the quality of the discussion on a particular topic, also provided the mental stimulation I needed.

As with all other pleasurable activities and situations, indulgence in books was not enough to keep me stable all the time. One morning, I returned from the supermarket and went straight to the chest freezer. It was already quite full, and as I shifted some items to create space for the ice cream and other frozen food I had just bought, I noticed a few bags from our domestic helper's stash, which her friends occasionally gave her, or which she sometimes cooked for herself. She was aware that I had no problem with her keeping her food in the freezer, but at times, there were quite a few packages that did not seem to dwindle. So, that morning, I gently reminded her to start consuming her food, and more frequently, as I needed the space. She lashed out, saying that I could not possibly expect her to finish so much in such a short time, and what did I expect... Stunned, and speaking softly, I asked why she had to speak to me so aggressively, when all I did was ask a valid question, and nicely, too. She chuckled, apologised, and said she was joking, before going to my daughter's room to finish cleaning.

Standing at the entrance to the kitchen, breathing slowly and deeply, I looked across the dining room towards the balcony. I was done. I was a failure. I could not look after my family without a domestic helper, but at the same time, I could no longer cope with another round of interviews, and training them in cooking and cleaning my way, in the hope that they would work out, and that I would want them to stay. No more helpers, no more chores, just no more, I stared at the balcony for a few seconds. It beckoned – a short turn to my right, and this would be over.

As my breathing became more rapid, I turned away and marched towards my room, barging through the door, and shutting it behind me, sobbing. My husband stepped off the exercise machine and asked what happened. She must go, I said. I know you think she is a fabulous helper, and she is, but she can't talk to me like that. I was barely coherent when I told him what had happened. It was not the first time; she had been rude to me on numerous occasions, all of which I had ignored because I liked her and wanted to keep her. My husband reminded me that she was one of the best helpers we had ever employed, and if I was sure I wanted to go through the whole process again. Getting hysterical by then, I shook my head, refusing to even consider another helper. I cannot deal with this, I said. My husband immediately went to the kitchen and told the helper that things were not working out for me and that she should look for another employer. He also told her she could take as much time as she wanted. She chose to stay for another week before going home.

My friends, many of whom had domestic helpers, assured me that finding and keeping a good helper was a problem for many people they knew, including themselves. Some of them lasted longer because employers were either very tolerant, or took a more detached approach to managing their household, or had no clue what their helpers were up to, or, more likely, a bit of each. I had learnt to be more tolerant, which is why the last helper had stayed for over a year. But on that very day, I was so affected by her response, and, instead of dismissing it as I had been doing in the previous instances, I reacted. Like Anthony Bourdain had said, *"It's an insignificant thing, it's a small thing, it's a hamburger, but it's not a good one. Suddenly, I look at the hamburger and I find myself in a spiral of depression that can last for days."* It was a small thing, but on that day, I reacted in a big way.

Had I succumbed to the urge, and taken just a few steps towards the balcony, it would have been over. But on the spur of the moment, I had stepped towards my left, towards the bedroom, towards my husband. I am glad I did.

Chapter 23

In his ground-breaking book, *The Definition of Suicide*,[1] the highly respected suicidologist, Dr. Edwin S. Shneidman, explored the nature of suicide and sought to help doctors to first identify patients who are suicidal, understand them, and treat them appropriately. He created a list of 10 characteristics commonly found in suicide, and, in the process, provided insights into a suicidal person's very being – thoughts, emotions, attitudes, wants, needs, actions, and inner stresses. Drawing lessons from his study of suicide notes, along with philosophy and literature, Dr. Shneidman's book offers a deep understanding of what drives a person to suicide.

According to Dr. Shneidman, suicide can be prevented primarily through education. He believed that the public needed to understand that suicide can happen to anyone, that the warning signs are identifiable, and that a suicidal person has access to help. His 10 characteristics – widely known as The Ten Commonalities of Suicide and still practised by doctors today – are outlined as the purpose, goal, stimulus, stressor, emotion, internal attitude, cognitive state, action, interpersonal act and consistency.

---

1   Published by Wiley-Interscience, 1985.

When I told my doctor at IMH that I had just begun writing a book about suicide, he mentioned Dr. Shneidman's book and the ten commonalities,[2] which Dr. Shneidman developed as part of his suicide prevention programme. I searched and found the following:

1. The common purpose of suicide is to seek a solution: A suicidal person is seeking a solution to a problem that is "generating intense suffering" within him or her.

2. The common goal of suicide is cessation of consciousness: The anguished mind of a suicidal person interprets the end of consciousness as the only way to end the suffering.

3. The common stimulus of suicide is psychological pain: Shneidman calls it "psychache," by which he means "intolerable emotion, unbearable pain, unacceptable anguish."

4. The common stressor in suicide is frustrated psychological needs: A suicidal person feels pushed toward self-destruction by psychological needs that are not being met (for example, the need for achievement, for nurturance or for understanding).

5. The common emotion in suicide is hopelessness-helplessness: A suicidal person feels despondent, utterly unsalvageable.

6. The common cognitive state of suicide is ambivalence: Suicidal people, Shneidman says, "wish to die and they simultaneously wish to be rescued."

7. The common perceptual state in suicide is constriction: The mind of a suicidal person is constricted in its ability

---

2   The Suicidal Mind, E.S. Shneidman, Oxford University Press, 1996.

to perceive options, and, in fact, mistakenly sees only two choices – either continue suffering or die.

8. The common action in suicide is escape: Shneidman calls it "the ultimate egression (another word for escape) besides which running away from home, quitting a job, deserting an army, or leaving a spouse... pale in comparison."

9. The common interpersonal act in suicide is communication of intention: "Many individuals intent on committing suicide... emit clues of intention, signals of distress, whimpers of helplessness, or pleas for intervention."

10. The common pattern in suicide is consistent with life-long styles of coping: A person's past tendency for black-and-white thinking, escapism, control, capitulation and the like could serve as a clue to how he or she might deal with a present crisis.

When I read this list, I immediately questioned the veracity of some of the characteristics, in particular two – ambivalence and the communication of intention. Dr. Shneidman wrote this list for suicides in general, without making a distinction between those escaping anguish from a mental illness and those escaping a dire situation, for example, huge financial debt. Having researched numerous suicides by those known to have had a mental illness, and reflecting on instances of my own suicidal ideation, there was no hint of ambivalence – they chose suicide methods and timings which would prevent a rescue – nor communication of intent. The decedents were determined to die. Families and friends left behind as a result of a suicide by a person who had been diagnosed with a mental disorder would assert there was never any sign. Speaking for myself, I was certainly not ambivalent the first time I tried to kill myself, and am unlikely to be, if ever I found myself on the brink of death again. It was not as if Kate Spade or Anthony Bourdain or numerous others who killed themselves had hoped someone would come in and cut the rope from which they hanged themselves.

Throughout my episodes of feeling suicidal over the years, especially in the last few when I was responsible for my mother, I rescued myself not because I wanted to, but because I felt more strongly about having to live than choosing to die. There is quite a difference in wanting to live and having to live – the former is a choice made freely, the latter is a choice forced upon the conscience. As for communicating an intention, it has never happened in my case, and is unlikely to. Again, this is quite different from telling my husband that I am feeling suicidal and need to see a doctor, at which point, I am not ready to act on my emotions. If ever that time comes again – and I hope it never does – the response would be much the same as in similar suicides all over the world, where loved ones would insist that "there were no signs".

Dr. Shneidman's list of the ten commonalities are not limited to suicides as a result of mental disorders. While the link between suicide and mental disorders,[3] in particular, depression and alcohol abuse, is well-substantiated in high-income countries, many suicides are also impulsive and happen at critical points, when a person is unable to cope with an extremely stressful situation, such as relationship or financial problems, or unbearable physical pain and illness.

3   World Health Organisation fact sheet https://www.who.int/news-room/fact-sheets/detail/suicide

Also adding to suicidal behaviour are factors including but not limited to, war, abuse, violence, bereavement and a sense of isolation. Discrimination against vulnerable groups, such as refugees and migrants; lesbian, gay, bisexual, transgender, (LGBT) persons; and prisoners, have been cited as reasons for suicide within this group.

Suicide is a global phenomenon, with over 80% of global suicides occurring in low- and middle-income countries in 2016.[4]

In recent years, reports on suicide, both online and in print, are usually accompanied by a suicide prevention hotline number. The World Health Organisation refers to suicide as a serious global public health issue,[5] being among the top 20 leading causes of death worldwide, with more deaths due to suicide than malaria, breast cancer, or war and homicide. Suicide is preventable, yet despite being a global public health issue, fewer than 50 countries[6] have a stand-alone national suicide prevention strategy adopted by the government. While some of these countries – England, Scotland, Sweden – have reported significant progress in reducing suicides, there are no figures to compare suicide rates amongst the mentally ill against those who kill themselves for a variety of other reasons besides mental illness.

I believe suicide prevention measures are highly likely to be more effective for those who do not really want to die, but who may not be able to find another way out, than for those who really do not wish to live any longer. Yet, for all the programmes

---

4   World Health Organisation fact sheet https://www.who.int/news-room/fact-sheets/detail/suicide

5   World Health Organisation, Publications / Overview / Suicide In The World. September 2019.

6   MiNDbank, published in November 2018, WHO National Suicide Prevention Strategies. Singapore is not amongst these countries.

on suicide prevention, for all the effort and funding that are channelled towards such programmes, suicide prevention relies largely on a suicidal person asking for help. With the stigma surrounding mental illness and suicide, countless lives will be lost simply because those who need help will not seek it for fear of being stigmatised.

Stigma is not an issue for me, and never has been. If ever I decide to kill myself, I would not call a hotline; the last thing I would want is prevention. As in my previous attempt, I went to great lengths to ensure that I did not send out any warning signs. According to numerous reports of high-profile suicides, particularly amongst those with a known mental disorder, even close friends and family members never saw any sign of distress in the weeks, days or even hours before a suicide. This deliberate, calculated effort to ensure a suicide will not be prevented, is what I believe makes the suicide difficult to understand for those left behind. Yet, for a person intent on escaping unbearable anguish, when death is more attractive than life, it is only reasonable to ensure that there are no obstacles to carrying out their plan. It is no wonder that a suicide that does not end in death is labelled a failed suicide, as was my experience in my first attempt, and which my husband prevented by the skin of his teeth. It had been meticulously planned but poorly executed, as I had not allowed for the possibility of my husband returning an hour earlier. If ever I found myself absolutely ready to kill myself – in the absence of any ambivalence – I would have to consider every possible detail to prevent a failed attempt once again.

Chapter 24

One of my generation's worst years is coming to a close, with some countries still reeling from the pandemic, and others seeing fast rising numbers. But there is hope yet, with vaccines showing signs of effectiveness. If anything, what this pandemic has taught me, specifically with the sheer numbers involved, is that life is what it has always been: fragile and unpredictable. It has also shown me that people are who we have always been, not always one or the other, and more likely the sum of a few parts, with most of my friends being all kind, caring, and loving, but there are also people who are inconsiderate, selfish and hateful. I have always valued some of my friendships, and the kinship with my husband and children, but never have I treasured these bonds of family and friends more than I have during this year, 2020. Having courted death, or even the idea of suicide, frequently, over a mere eight months, I can safely credit them for keeping me alive.

It is an impossible goal for me to remain in a perpetually non-suicidal state. To stay alive, I must then try to minimise my suicidal phases. My past experiences with triggers have taught me what to avoid, and consequently, what to cherish regardless of how I feel. Avoiding people and situations which cause me anxiety or pain is not something I am good at, often taking action only after a bad experience.

Creating calming and rewarding experiences for myself is something I learnt to do only in the past few years. Some days when I find myself alone in the living room, I listen to music, usually from the '70s, doing nothing else but focussing on the songs. Some days I bake a cake, usually a simple lemon drizzle or orange loaf, which I then slice and freeze. Or I bake shortbread, a jar of which is scoffed within two days. Often, I think of the people – friends, former colleagues, acquaintances – with whom I have shared memorable experiences, some of whom go as far back to my secondary school days.

I have also found contentment and satisfaction as a volunteer with Transient Workers Count Too, also known as TWC2, a non-governmental organisation dedicated to promoting equitable treatment of migrant workers in Singapore. Inspired by Debbie Fordyce, TWC2's president and herself a volunteer, a few volunteers and I gather on the first Monday evening of every month, at a room in a small lane off Serangoon Road, to issue meal cards to destitute migrant workers who are waiting for outcomes on their injury claims and salary disputes. These men, mostly from Bangladesh and India, are typically in distress and as victims of exploitation by unscrupulous employers, must fight for what is due to them. TWC2 case workers help them with their claims, while volunteers like me do the administration of meal cards to ensure they do not go hungry. Even after almost five years of volunteering with TWC2, I have found it difficult to detach myself from the misery forced upon these men. Yet, my sadness for them stops at a point long before it turns into depression for me. Much bigger than this sadness is the emotional reward of speaking to them, seeing them smile, and express gratitude either with a nod or a simple "thank you", when volunteers wish them, with all sincerity, the very best outcome, as we hand over their meal cards.

There are still many unknowns – triggers that I cannot predict – but I do what I can to help myself. Sleep being critical to my state of mind, I no longer hesitate to take a 25mg dosage of quetiapine, even if it leaves me feeling dull and listless for part of the next day. My friendships mean the world to me, and where I was once afraid of setting boundaries with certain friends for fear of jeopardising the friendship, I am no longer afraid to do so.

It is almost always the little things that set me off, rarely ever the big and the obvious. Which is what makes it so hard for people to understand. How can something so inconsequential lead to suicide? Especially for someone who seems to have it all – a husband, children, and friends who are all kind and loyal, a beautiful home, and a comfortable life? Because that "small thing" makes itself big in a troubled mind, causing unbearable anguish. Just as it is the little things that can set me off on a downward spiral, it is equally the little things that can lift my spirits and give me yet another reason to stay alive.

In 2004, the world-renowned Taiwanese-American journalist and writer, Iris Chang, celebrated for her best-selling book, *The Rape of Nanking*, a searing account of the Nanking Massacre, was found dead in her car from a self-inflicted gunshot. She was 36 years old, and had been diagnosed with bipolar disorder two weeks before her death. Months earlier, she had admitted herself into a psychiatric hospital. Three notes, dated the day before she died, were found later, one of which struck a responsive chord with me:

I promise to get up and get out of the house every morning. I will stop by to visit my parents then go for a long walk. I will follow the doctor's orders for medications. I promise not to hurt myself. I promise not to visit Web sites that talk about suicide.

I had chanced upon this note while reading about Iris Chang. At that time, my husband was away in Ethiopia and I thought it might be a good tool to help me prevent my own suicide. I copied and pasted all the words, replacing "visit my parents", with "call my mother", and deleted the line about following doctor's orders, about which I was diligent anyway. I then emailed it to myself to read every time suicide ideation hit me. But within months of feeling suicidal a few times, the words were futile, just as they had been for Iris Chang. The promises felt childish and trivial. I deleted the email.

A few months ago, at the beginning of circuit breaker Phase 1, I devised some steps to help myself change my suicidal mind – from an absolute belief in death as my salvation, to knowing that my suicidal mind is transient. For this to happen, my suicidal mind, already tumultuous, would also need to recognise and accept the consequences of my suicide. This was usually the case, anyway, but there were times in the past when I was not able to think about consequences, and my mind focused on nothing but suicide. In the event that my suicidal ideation went from passive to active, I had a plan to allow myself a way out: my last meal would include one hawker food, which would vary depending on the time; a slice of cake, again, depending on the time; and I must smoke five sticks of cigarettes. Hawker food, especially chicken rice, is usually available until late at night. Cake shops may not always be open, but I always have cake in the freezer. I do not have cigarettes at home, which means I must go out to get a pack. With so many steps involved, I felt I could prevent my suicide if ever I got to that stage; it was possible, likely even, that in the process of going to the hawker centre, or the cake shop, or to get cigarettes, I might change my mind. If not, then the time spent trying to smoke five sticks of cigarettes, might help me change my mind.

Since drawing up these steps, I have felt suicidal several times. Each time, I have taken a slice of cake out of the freezer and let it thaw for about 20 minutes. This deliberate action of waiting to eat my favourite food would force me to think about whether or not I really wanted to die. Sometimes, the answer is yes, I do, and sometimes it is no, I do not. But every time, I tell myself, I must not. I cannot. I should not. I repeat this like a mantra, perhaps three or four times. With my thoughts occupied by my husband and children, and my close friends, the urge usually dissipates.

Just when I believe that everything is going to be just fine, that all the little things that have ever given rise to suicidal ideation have either disappeared or no longer bother me, one thing or another would crop up. Starting from late November, we began to hear television sounds in our living room at around 10 o'clock at night, after we had switched off our television.

We listened on the walls, and could not tell if the cinematic sounds were from our next-door neighbour, or the people upstairs. I went to listen outside their doors. It was from upstairs, and we assumed they had bought a new television set with a powerful sound system. We wrote to them, explaining the problem and asked if they could try placing some insulation between their new appliance and the wall or floor. There was no change. Let's give it a few days, my husband said. Maybe they haven't checked their mailbox. A few days turned into nearly two weeks. It was unpleasant to be in our living room having a family conversation with the sound from their television filling our room.

I begged my husband to speak to them, to tell them we were not being difficult, and ask them to please come downstairs to our flat and just listen for themselves. If they thought we were being unreasonable, we would let the matter rest. Reluctantly, he went upstairs, while I went to our room, unable to face them. From there, I heard the woman shouting, and picked up on the word "harass". I was stunned, and waited for my husband to return. The man had been okay, he said, but the woman, who was lying on her sofa, told her husband to shut the door because she did not want to be harassed. As my husband recounted the event, which barely lasted half a minute, I trembled, trying to process her words and her tone. I had not expected such a hostile response to what we believed was a reasonable request.

I apologised to my husband for sending him upstairs, and asked him, what kind of person creates such an unpleasant living environment for a neighbour, and when told about it, along with a plea to be a little more quiet, turns things around and claims harassment? Aren't we the ones who have been harassed for more than six years? My husband shrugged; except for the woman's claim of harassment, their refusal to come to our flat was the outcome he had expected. To be fair, he reminded me, apart from things sometimes being dropped on the floor late at night and early in the morning, they have been reasonably quiet during the day for the past few years. Yes, they have, I protested, but peace and quiet is what neighbours should expect from each other. It's what everyone in our neighbourhood gets. I wanted to say, I don't know for how long more I can take this, but I did not want to alarm him.

While my husband went to speak to our daughter, who was working from home late into the night, I went out onto the balcony and looked below at the shrubs lit by warm yellow lights. I had always said that I would never jump from a building, for fear of landing on and killing an innocent passer-by. This was not a problem from my balcony. I had made a mental note soon after we moved in that I would not jump from our flat, because I would land on shrubs on the ground floor, which would lead to me sustaining extensive and permanent damage, but not death. I took a deep breath and walked to the side of the balcony, and below was the tiled patio of the ground floor flat. I had not noticed it before, and stared at it, envisioning myself going head down. Dead, for sure, I told myself. I jumped back, horrified at such a thought. The woman's shrill voice and her noxious words flowed rapidly through my mind, back and forth, like wild waves pounding against rocks.

The woman's bathroom light came on. I shuddered and walked quickly to join my husband and daughter in her makeshift office. I sat on the bed, half-listening to them, half-buried in my thoughts from moments earlier. *I shall not, I must not kill myself.*

Even with the steps I had introspectively drawn up, it is possible for me to forget them, or ignore them, if I get to the point where I feel so tormented that I can no longer bear the thought of living. This is when my salvation from death far outweighs any possible reason I could have for remaining alive – my husband, my children, my friends. I have been in that state before, and in the crucial moments, I devoted much thought to my beloved husband and children, and told myself that I could not allow them to live with the consequences of my suicide. And yet, I had proceeded to kill myself, only to be rescued. Because sometimes, for some people, suicide is very seductive, even when life seems as perfect as it can be, as if it could not be any better.

As deeply as I believe that I should not kill myself, I cannot be sure that I will not act on a suicide ideation, whether it lasts for minutes or for days. I will never know or predict when a situation is about to cause me anguish so extreme that I shut my mind down, unable to think rationally, abandoning all thoughts of suicide prevention, only to focus on death as my salvation. It could be impulsive, or meticulously planned. It could be triggered by something small, or something that has brewed for a long time. It will be unpredictable even to me, in my volatile mind.

The new year is less than two weeks away. Phase 3 of circuit breaker was just announced, along with news that all citizens and long-term residents will be voluntarily vaccinated by the end of 2021. Things are already looking better. In my mind, I have already left behind this year, along with all its wretchedness. At the same time, I have treasured all the goodness that has flourished, and will take them with me into the next year and beyond. It will be a spectacular year.

For now, and for the future, the promise I had made to my husband after my failed attempt – to never try suicide again – is the one that I plan, and fervently hope, to always keep. Meanwhile, I shall continue to live my enchanted life surrounded by the love of my incredible family and friends.

The End

List of Selected Suicides

Name	Age	Mental Disorder	Method	Year
Cleomenes I, Agiad King of Sparta		Insanity	Self-mutilation	490 B.C.
Brita Horn, Swedish. Countess and courtier	46	Long period of melancholy*	Drowning	1791
Amy Levy, British. Poet and novelist	27	Depression	Carbon monoxide poisoning	1889
Vincent van Gogh	37	Manic depressive illness**	Gunshot	1890
Ludwig Boltzmann, German physicist and philosopher	62	Manic depressive illness** (based on symptoms)	Hanging	1906
Prince Joachim of Prussia	29	Depression	Gunshot	1920
Wallace Carothers, American inventor of nylon	41	Depression	Potassium cyanide	1937
Virginia Woolf	59	Manic depressive illness**	Drowning	1941
Alan Turing, British mathematician, father of theoretical computer science and artificial intelligence	54	Depression (suspected)	Cyanide	1941
Osamu Dazai, Japanese writer	38	Depression	Drowning	1948

Name	Age	Mental Disorder	Method	Year
Sadegh Hedayat, Iranian intellectual	48	Depression	Carbon monoxide poisoning	1951
Ernest Hemmingway	62	Depression (Manic depressive illness**)	Gunshot	1961
Marilyn Monroe, American actress	36	Anxiety and depression	Barbiturates overdose	1962
Diana Churchill, daughter of Winston Churchill	54	Nervous breakdown	Barbiturates overdose	1963
Sylvia Plath, American poet and novelist	30	Chronic depression (generally believed to be bipolar disorder)	Carbon monoxide poisoning	1963
Frederick Fleet, British sailor and Titanic survivor	77	Depression	Hanging	1965
Anne Sexton, American Pulitzer-prize winning poet	45	Manic depressive illness**	Carbon monoxide poisoning	1974
Kari Kairamo, Finnish. Chairman & CEO, Nokia	56	Bipolar disorder (suspected)	Hanging	1988
Abbie Hoffman, American. Proponent of the Flower Power movement and one of the Chicago Seven	52	Bipolar disorder	Overdose of phenobarbital	1989
Capucine, French model and actress	62	Depression	Jumped from her apartment	1990

Name	Age	Mental Disorder	Method	Year
Gu Cheng, Chinese poet and novelist	37	Depression	Hanging	1993
Roy Raymond, American founder of Victoria's Secrets	46	Depression (suspected)	Jumped off the Golden Gate Bridge	1993
Kurt Cobain, American musician	27	Bipolar disorder	Gunshot	1994
Hai Zi, Chinese poet	25	Depression	Laid on a railway track	1989
Lembit Oll, Estonian chess grandmaster	33	Depression	Jumped out of building	1999
Leslie Cheung, Hong Kong actor	46	Depression	Jumped from hotel rooftop	2003
Iris Chang, American writer	36	Bipolar disorder	Gunshot	2004
Isabella Blow, British magazine editor	48	Depression	Herbicide	2007
Tiffany Simelane. Swazi beauty queen	21	Depression (suspected)	Pesticide	2009
Alexander McQueen, British fashion designer	40	Anxiety and depressive disorder	Hanging	2010
Peu Sousa, Brazilian guitarist	35	Depression	Hanging	2013
L'Wren Scott, American stylist and girlfriend of Mick Jagger	49	Depression	Hanging	2014

Name	Age	Mental Disorder	Method	Year
Andreas Lubitz, German pilot & mass murderer due to method of suicide	27	Psychotic depression	Deliberately crashing Germanwings Flight 9525	2015
Kimi Qiao Renliang, Chinese actor and singer	28	Depression	Self-inflicted wounds	2016
Chris Cornell, musician	52	Depression	Hanging	2017
Avicii, Swedish, superstar DJ and musician	28	Anxiety, depression, addiction	Self-inflicted wounds (broken glass)	2018
Kate Spade, designer	55	Anxiety and depression	Hanging	2018
Anthony Bourdain, celebrity chef	61	Depression	Hanging	2018
Kushal Punjabi, Indian actor	42	Depression	Hanging	2019
Yang Yang, Chinese opera star and music professor	44	Depression	Jumped from a building	2019

*Now known as depression   **Now known as bipolar disorder

Acknowledgements

Writing this book was agonising, but it also reminded me of how fortunate I am to be surrounded by the family and friends I have. I am indebted to them.

To my husband, a most kind, loyal and solid giant of a man, and our wonderful daughters, my angels. Thank you for your absolute love and support, for always looking out for me, and for indulging me in innumerable ways.

To my friends, old and new, near and far. Thank you for your kindnesss, thoughtfulness and patience, especially while I struggled. I count myself lucky.

To Dr Bhanu Gupta, a most intuitive and compassionate psychiatrist at the Institute of Mental Health. Thank you for your care, which has allowed me to maintain phases of stability.

To Joshua Ip, thank you for encouraging me to proceed with this book when I had doubts.

To my publisher, Marshall Cavendish, thank you for publishing this book.

About the Author

Mahita Vas was diagnosed with Type 1 bipolar disorder in 2005, after more than 20 years of struggling with mood swings and suicidal ideation. As a mental health advocate, she speaks candidly about mental health. She is also a volunteer with Transient Workers Count Too. She has written three books, including a memoir on mental illness. This is her fourth book. Mahita is married and has twin daughters in their late twenties.